CONCILIUM

THEOLOGY IN THE AGE OF RENEWAL

CONCILIUM

CONCILIUM/VOL. 20

SCRIPTURE

THE
DYNAMISM
OF
BIBLICAL
TRADITION

Volume 20

CONCILIUM
theology in the age of renewal

PAULIST PRESS
NEW YORK, N.Y. / GLEN ROCK, N.J.

NIHIL OBSTAT: Joseph F. Donahue, S.J., S.T.L.
Censor Deputatus

IMPRIMATUR: ✠ Bernard J. Flanagan, D.D.
Bishop of Worcester

November 29, 1966

Library of Congress Catalogue Card Number: 67-15983

Suggested Decimal Classification: 291.8

BOOK DESIGN: Claude Ponsot

Paulist Press assumes responsibility for the accuracy of the English translations in this Volume.

PAULIST PRESS
EXECUTIVE OFFICES: 304 W. 58th Street, New York, N.Y. and 21 Harristown Road, Glen Rock, N.J.
Executive Publisher: John A. Carr, C.S.P.
Executive Manager: Alvin A. Illig, C.S.P.
Asst. Executive Manager: Thomas E. Comber, C.S.P.

EDITORIAL OFFICES: 304 W. 58th Street, New York, N.Y.
Editor: Kevin A. Lynch, C.S.P.
Managing Editor: Urban P. Intondi

Printed and bound in the United States of America by
The Colonial Press Inc., Clinton, Mass.

CONTENTS

Preface

Pierre Benoit, O.P./*Jerusalem, Jordan*

Roland E. Murphy, O.Carm./*Washington, D.C.*

Bastiaan van Iersel, S.M.M./*Nijmegen, Netherlands*

When the bible is viewed primarily as the revelation of God, its content receives most of our attention, and we forget that the bible is also a witness—a witness to man's struggle for truth, to his seeking God in history. But as soon as we take note of the human dimensions of scripture, and especially how it came into being, a new perspective opens. We appreciate not merely the content, but also the manner in which that content was formulated within the People of God throughout its long history. We recognize the long road traveled by Israel toward true faith and acknowledgment of God, and we find an example that inspires us in our own journey.

The dynamism of biblical tradition is particularly relevant today because it can help us better understand the role which tradition must have in the Church. Too often we have lost sight of the fact that what has been transmitted (tradition in the passive sense) is itself a living reality and not dead and unchanging. Precisely through the study of the traditions contained in the bible we capture the continual development that goes on. There are many reasons for this development, but the primary one is the fact that biblical traditions are subject to the laws of history. They also have an inner bond of unity—for example, the firm belief that God gives redemption and salvation to man by his action in history and in nature. But however this unifying belief

1

is to be described, there is an inevitable diversity in its formulation because this is done by different people in ever-changing situations.

This general thesis is developed concretely by Pierre Grelot in the opening article. Both the Old and the New Testaments are seen to be the distillation of a whole complex of data that is far more than a mere handing down of words; these are traditions that live and develop. The seven articles which follow work this out in greater detail in the light of a single theme or text.

Joseph Schreiner writes about the ancient Israelite *credo*. Originally it was a liturgical proclamation of Yahweh as the God of Israel who revealed himself in history, but later it was expanded to refer to the God who also reveals himself in nature. This creed never became so fixed that it failed to remain open to the ongoing development. There is a certain tension between this article and that of Joseph Blenkinsopp, who takes up the creed once more in order to show how the exile enriched the old confession of faith.

Raymond Tournay leads us into the post-exilic period, when the Israelite sages wrote in the style of "anthological composition". They used the vocabulary and phraseology of the canonical books of the Law and prophets to form a theological synthesis with new emphases; for example, never before did the idea of creation play so important a role in the religious thought of Israel.

Frans Neirynck concentrates on the unusual text of Mark 9, 33-50, and shows how the separate sayings ("logia") of Jesus take on a new dimension when they are worked together into a mosaic.

Joseph Fitzmyer goes back to the Old Testament and pre-Christian Judaism in order to illustrate the development of the theme of the Son of David (Mt. 22, 41-46). David Stanley's study of the earliest preaching (Acts 1-13) focuses upon the basic notions which also figure in other layers of the early tradition. Jules Cambier analyzes St. Paul and illustrates both the perduring aspect of tradition (loyalty to the Lord and to the

Gospel) as well as its dynamic aspect (Paul's loyalty to the Spirit which is at work in the Church of Christ).

The topic of the bibliographical survey is the homily, an important expression of the theme of this issue of *Concilium*, because tradition has not come to an end; it is still going on, as in the pronouncements of the Church's magisterium and in the work of theologians. For the faithful tradition is at work and alive in the liturgical proclamation, especially in the homily or sermon. The successful homily re-presents and actualizes the old texts so that they become God's living Word for our time. Although it is not identical with the Word spoken by God through the prophets and apostles, it is in continuity with it.

It is clear therefore that it is not only *what* the scriptures say that is important for our faith, but also the *way* in which they were written. This insight will affect our formulation of the faith, our preaching, our proclamation and our theology. We cannot mark time, or simply use the same old terminology; we must go forward in continuity with the traditions to which the People of God bore witness by its proclamation and belief, both during and after the period in which the scriptures were written.

PART I
ARTICLES

Pierre Grelot / *Paris, France*

Tradition as Source and Environment of Scripture

For a long time theology has treated the problem of the relations between scripture and tradition only as a question of the relations between a scripture already *fixed* in its canonical composition and an *ecclesiastical* tradition inheriting the authority of the apostles. Such was the case in the Protestant-Catholic controversy or in the discussion among Catholic theologians about "the two sources of revelation". But the problem also deserves to be examined at another level: that of the living tradition in which scripture found both its source and its living environment. I propose to study this point in the two Testaments, reserving a special place for Christ at the point where these two meet.

I

P. H. Menoud has said: "The Old Testament does not know about the idea of tradition. . . . To set up a tradition in the framework of the covenant of promise is to introduce purely human views into the history of salvation whose development God foresaw and for which he laid out the plan; it arbitrarily adds to a given situation whose sole legitimate complement is Jesus Christ. That is why Jesus rejects the tradition of the ancients as a man-made tradition." [1] Is this a defense of the *scriptura sola*?

[1] Cf. his article, "Tradition," in *Vocabulaire biblique*, ed. J. J. von Allmen (Neuchâtel-Paris, 1954), p. 294; Eng. tr.: *Companion to the Bible* (Oxford, 1958).

This verdict is probably better explained in the article on "Para-dosis" in Kittel's *Theologisches Wörterbuch,* which points out that if we make it a matter of vocabulary there is indeed no word in the Septuagint that corresponds to the word in question. But is this enough for a full understanding of the biblical reality? In that case the idea of promise would also be absent from the Old Testament because Hebrew has no particular word to express it. But what kind of conclusion could one draw from that? The question, therefore, demands another approach. The role of tradition in the ancient Eastern religions will provide a useful point of comparison.

1. *Tradition in the Ancient Eastern Religions*

In the ancient East religion is intimately linked up with the structures of the human society that practices it. Hence, it is subject to the repercussions of events that change the face of such a society. This happened when Cyrus took Babylon and when Alexander set out on his conquests. Yet, this development of various cults is less important than their universal continuity. This is because these religions were not *historical* religions, established by historical founders like the Buddha or Mohammed (except, perhaps, in the case of the reform of Zoroaster, which is a problem). These religions were *traditional* religions whose origin lies buried in the darkness of time and whose syncretic nature easily adjusts itself to the accidents of history. In an age when the religious and social elements are completely integrated, their contents cover every field of existence. Their beliefs and representations, organized into more or less complicated mythologies, their rituals and prayer formulas, their technical procedures for divination and magic—all these factors tend to get fixed in gestures and texts that regulate religious thought and action. The transmission of this complex material creates a factual tradition closely linked up with the level of civilization and the structures of society itself.

During a first stage these myths and rites are entrusted to a live memory which occupies a privileged place in every social group: in the family group, clan or tribe and in the specialist groups of functionaries or priests. At a later stage, the appearance of systems of writing create a more perfect support for the live memory to do its job. It is under these conditions that people collected the great myths, the rituals (where many rubrics are left out!), the prayer formulas, the oracles, etc. It is a fortunate accident that these texts have come down to us while other similar religions have disappeared forever. But the fact that there was a written literature, varying in importance according to the case, did not prevent the living tradition from continuing to exist in its oral forms and practices, along with the written form, as the life-giving environment to which the literary expression was subordinated and from which the written form drew its main elements. No doubt, the vicissitudes of history occasionally brought about brutal interruptions or introduced elements that transformed the tradition. But the conquerors themselves were anxious to encourage the worship they found in the sanctuaries of the countries they conquered so that the religious tradition could carry on without difficulty. This is what happened in Babylon after the conquests of Cyrus and in Egypt after those of Alexander.

2. *Religious Tradition in the Old Testament*

In this general situation the religion of Israel shows a feature that is undeniably new, not only in its monotheism but also in the importance attached to the *Word of God,* of which the prophets (in the broad sense) are the custodians. Because of this, the religious values proper to Israel cannot be considered traditional in the sense in which this is understood in other religions. These values appear in history at a definite date, through those that were the witnesses of the divine revelation. "Your fathers lived of old beyond the Euphrates . . . and served other gods. . . . Then I took your father Abraham from beyond the river. . . ." (Jos. 24, 2ff.). Thus the Old Testament started off with a radical reform of the preceding religious tradition, based on a prophetic experience accorded to the father of the race. Later on, the Word of God continued to mark the course of events of which the main ones can be located in history. Having become a historical event through the prophets, it joins up by the same token with that other basic fact which lies at the root of faith: the sequence of historical experiences in which the prophets invited the people to see God's plan. And so, the two elements that give Israel's religion its own specific character are the message of the prophets, who are seen as the bearers of God's Word, and sacred history, which is seen as the manifestation of God's deeds.

Yet, the subject of this message and this historical experience is not a heap of individuals. It is the *People of God,* an organized community, at once temporal and religious, a people whose path one can trace from the age of the patriarchs to that of the New Testament. In the course of the centuries its structures underwent many changes, from the nomadic clans and the federation of twelve tribes down to the theocratic period during the Persian era and the kingdom of Herod under the protection of the Roman Empire. But underneath these changes on the surface, the religious calling of Israel bestowed a unique meaning on the society affected by them: Israel is the People of God, the holy nation (Exod. 19, 5-6; Deut. 7, 6), called to serve God in the practice of its worship, in observing his commandments, in realizing God's design in history and bearing witness to him before the world. But how can we speak of a *People of God* without evoking at the same time the *living tradition* of that human community whose whole existence carries a meaning determined by the Word of God? Every aspect of its social life is integrated in this meaning: its family life, its civic institutions, its wars as well as its worship.

The Word of God produced undoubted changes in all these aspects, compared to the customs of earlier traditions. However, each aspect still showed inner threads of continuity attaching the usages and customs of Israel to those of the surrounding communities—e.g., their religious rites and phraseology. Also, each Word of God and the change it brought became a sacred deposit; this was built up into a tradition which was then handed on. Therefore, the Word of God and the deeds of God were at the same time makers of tradition and objects of tradition.

Here one ought to examine the various *milieux* where this tradition is preserved and the various functions that have to protect it. The sociology of each period would here provide various indications. The family has always been an especially appropriate center for the transmission of rites, customs and beliefs and for the remembrance of sacred history (Exod. 12, 26-27; 13, 14-15). But the tribes and their full assembly (cf. Jos. 24), the administration of the centralized kingdom, the sanctuaries dispersed throughout the country, the national temple at Jerusalem, etc., are also of importance. The preservation of the heritage of the patriarchs, Moses and the prophets was indeed the principal task of the priests as custodians of law and worship, of the leaders and kings who were in charge of the nation's life, of the scribes to whom the wisdom of the ancestors was entrusted. In this there are clear parallels with all the religious traditions of the East. This does not mean that the Word of God was exposed to the hazards of a *purely human institution:* although the Spirit of God did not guarantee all these functionaries in the same degree as the prophets, he was not alien to their activity as long as they showed themselves docile in the exercise of these functions. The sacred historians say this occasionally about the leaders or the kings (Deut. 34, 9; Jg. 6, 11-40; 1 Sam. 10, 10; 11, 6); the cantors (1 Chr. 25, 1-3); and the scribes (Ecclus. 39, 1-9; 51, 13-26; Wis. 7, 15-21; 8, 21; 9, 17). Thus the tradition of the People of God, phased by the always unpredictable missions of the prophets, was also structured by the *charismatic functions* that protected the faithful preservation of its contents. If ambiguity still remained, it was due to the attitude adopted in practice by those that were charged with these functions.

3. *The Birth of Scripture in the Tradition*

The form assumed by Israel's tradition followed the evolution of Israel's culture. As elsewhere, we must reckon first of all with the oral tradition that existed before the use of writing and then along with it. For the period of the patriarchs this oral tradition was the only way of transmitting, according to Genesis. At the time of Moses, writing had a real, though limited, place: even if the "ten words" which laid down the charter of the covenant (Exod. 31, 18; 34, 28) were engraved on tables of stone, the existence of a levitical priesthood would be adequate for a long time for the preservation of law and worship, either by a practical introduction to the ritual or by memorizing the texts. Those were the conditions that presided over the development of the Mosaic legacy under the pressure of various needs, such as the application of the Torah to concrete cases in actual life, or the representation of remembered incidents of sacred history according to the needs of the age or of the people, or, again, the enrichment or regulation of the ritual after the settlement in Canaan and after the Babylonian captivity, etc. Thereafter, the written texts begin to appear, but their composition is literally immersed in the basic tradition that upholds them: it is there that they look for their principal material; they take over the literary forms even if they have to arrange them in order to adjust them to a new cultural context; they present the contents of that tradition in view of the spiritual needs of this or that age.

We apply critical methods to the Pentateuch so that we can reconstitute as far as possible the history of its composition by situating its various layers in time. When we do this, we are actually studying a particularly important facet of Israel's tradition until the definitive establishment of the Torah which probably coincides with the mission of Esdras. And if this work cannot be done without a certain amount of hesitation, on the other hand, it considerably enriches our knowledge of the People of God and our understanding of its writings. Once we know at what point these writings come into its history and into its social and institutional life, it becomes easier to acquire a correct appreciation of its literary forms and their bearing. At all events, this history of the Pentateuch is inextricably linked up with that of the other books: the historical books from Joshua to Kings, the prophetical books and the old collections of psalms and proverbs. In all these fields the establishment of a written text, which may

imply several successive stages, is always rooted in the oral tradition, the special laws of which cannot be ignored by scientific
criticism.

At the beginning of this century exegesis paid little attention to
this aspect. Since then a more exact knowledge of ancient civiliza-
tions and of the parallels provided by ethnology, a more penetrating study of the literary *genres* of the bible and their relationship to concrete environment where they were in use, have put
the question on a new basis. Here the work done by Scandinavian
exegetes since J. Pedersen, S. Mowinckel, H. S. Nyberg and
H. Birkeland should be mentioned. Between 1950 and 1960
I. Engnell of Sweden and E. Nielsen of Denmark[2] traced the
principal lines of this "traditional-historical method", or the critical study of the traditions. With an eye particularly on the transmission of *texts* at a certain level of civilization, they consider that
up to the Babylonian captivity Israel was a people with an essentially oral culture, writing being reserved to the practical needs
of commerce and administration. The matter contained in the
Pentateuch, the prophetical books and the ancient psalms would
therefore be preserved only by means of memorization methods.
We should therefore apply to them an analytical method which
befits the laws that govern an oral transmission and soft-pedal, or
even leave alone, the kind of classical literary approach in use
some fifty years ago. These suggestions were not universally accepted. In 1947 J. van der Ploeg was already examining them in
detail. More recently A. H. J. Gunneweg subjected them to a
penetrating study, limiting himself to the situation of the prophetical writings.[3]

It was surely useful to draw attention to the *fact of tradition*
with which we are confronted in the Old Testament. It would

[2] Cf. I. Engnell, "Traditionshistorisk Method," in *Svenskt Bibliskt
Uppslagsverk*, Vol. II (Stockholm, 1952), pp. 1429-37; E. Nielsen, *Oral
Tradition;* Eng. tr.: *Studies in Biblical Theology* 11 (London, 1954), with
bibliography.
[3] J. van der Ploeg, "Le rôle de la tradition orale dans la transmission du
texte de l'A.T.," in *Rev. Bibl.* 54 (1947), pp. 5-41; A. H. J. Gunneweg,
Mündliche und schriftliche Tradition der vorexilischen Propheten Bücher
(Göttingen, 1959).

be a pity to limit this aspect to the oral transmission of the *texts* at the expense of the *practical* elements that are as important as the texts themselves. But there is something more serious in this. When it is a matter of texts that by their very form are fixed, such as poetical texts, can one accept such a clean break between the oral composition and the written one, between oral preservation and written preservation? Would we not underrate the role of writing in Israel at the time of the kings if we confine the activity of the scribes of the temple or palace to merely practical business? Is it not exaggerating somewhat when one excludes classical literary criticism as if the traditions are adequate by themselves? In short, we ought to beware of opposing activities which in fact are complementary. It was necessary to expand the methods used at the beginning of this century and to make them more elastic. But since the genesis of oral literature, the oral preservation of established texts and the composition of written literature make up together the *total fact of tradition* which embraced all the features of life in Israel, exegesis should know how to make use of all the means offered by classical literary criticism, *Formgeschichte* and the criticism of traditions.

From the exile on, it is true that the situation developed. The quantity of sacred writings was by then sufficiently important to influence the authors in an increasingly perceptible manner. The use of the *anthological form*[4] shows that they had recourse to sources that can be identified. This is because the "men of the Book" replace more and more often the "men of the Word" as spiritual guides for the People of God. But by thus explaining the ancient writings for their time and suggesting that they should be reread [5] in a new perspective, they take their place in the chain of tradition that is enriched simultaneously by their oral teaching and their written work.

If we study the texts in that light, we shall respect at the same

[4] A. Robert, "Littéraires (Genres)," in *Dict. Bible Suppl.*, Vol. V, p. 411; "Le genre littéraire du Cantique des cantiques," in *Vivre et penser* 3 (Rev. Bibl., 1944), pp. 199ff.

[5] A. Gelin, "La question des 'relectures' bibliques à l'intérieur d'une tradition vivante," in *Sacra Pagina,* Vol. I Congress of Louvain (Gemboux-Paris, 1959), pp. 303-15.

time the personal character of scriptural inspiration and its social aspects because the activity of the sacred authors cannot be separated from their communal purpose. This general approach throws light on the special problem of the Septuagint, considered as the functional fulfillment of a specific need of Alexandrian Judaism. Faced with the Greek language and Greek thought, it had to find a way of expression that suited its cultural environment in order better to express the originality of its faith. As a legitimate witness of its communal life, its preaching and its theology, the Septuagint constitutes the basic document of one branch of the Jewish tradition under the undoubted charismatic guidance of the Holy Spirit. Nobody disagrees with this, even though many theologians refuse to go further and credit its inspiration.[6] These observations lead us to the threshold of the New Testament. By then the living tradition had become a complex reality, actively transmitted not only by the priests and doctors of the law but also by all those who shared in the preservation of the ancestral inheritance and the explanation of the scriptures, either in the context of preaching in the synagogue or in the composition of literary works of which we have only some remnants. Among the tendencies these men represent, there is not one that can claim to be by itself the sole representative of Jewish orthodoxy. From this point of view, Qumran belongs as much to the tradition as the old pharisaism, and Alexandrian literature as much as that of Palestine. It was in this context that Jesus appeared.

II

When the *Word made flesh* appears on the scene, the manifestation of God's Word to mankind and the achievement of God's deeds in history reach their apogee. The unexpected and unforeseeable, absolute and definitive character of that Word which God speaks to us in him places it in a situation by itself, for which there is no comparison. Nevertheless, his birth within

[6] Cf. my explanation in *La Bible, Parole de Dieu* (Tournai-Paris, 1965), pp. 166-74.

the Jewish people inserts him in the very heart of the tradition of Israel, and we must see what attitude he adopts toward it.

1. *Jesus and the Jewish Tradition*

Jesus' relation toward the Old Testament is expressed in terms of *fulfillment*. With him "the time is fulfilled" (Mk. 1, 15); the preparatory history has come to an end. But let us look carefully at the meaning of this statement. Israel's secular experience is in fact integrated in the living tradition of which scripture is a main ingredient. It is there that Jesus introduces the mysterious reality whose gradual manifestation will reveal the meaning of all that preceded. Hence, one can understand the two other aspects of the evangelical *fulfillment*: Jesus "fulfills the Law and the prophets" in all that concerns the conduct of life (Mt. 5, 17); in his human destiny "everything written about me in the law of Moses and the prophets and the psalms must be fulfilled" (Lk. 24, 44). If, on both these counts, the inspired texts are meant, these texts do not exist independently of the community that reads and interprets them in order to live by them. Now, it is in this situation that Jesus explains their meaning and bearing. In order to understand his attitude toward the scriptures, we therefore have to take into account the reading of the Law and the prophets in the synagogue, of which the Targums and Midrashim give us a glimpse (cf. Lk. 4, 16-21), and the use of the psalms in the temple and in the synagogue; in this liturgical setting the texts are given, according to the feasts, particular implications or shades of meaning about the deeds of God commemorated by these feasts and about the eschatological salvation that these feasts make the people hope for.[7] One must also take into account the theology preserved by the various branches of the Jewish tradition in more elaborate ways. Jesus was not bound by any of that because the *fulfillment* he brings surpasses all that Israel could imagine or expect. But he does not scorn it when he introduces an entirely new principle of interpretation.

---

[7] Cf., for example, the study by R. Le Déaut, *La nuit pascale,* Analecta biblica, 22 (Rome, 1963).

What is called the "tradition of the elders" (Mk. 7, 5) represents only a very limited aspect of the great tradition: namely,
the rabbinical *halacha* which is essentially based on the customary teaching of the doctors of the Law and ultimately linked up
with scripture by means of exegetical contrivances. Jesus explicitly compares the written law, which is the "Word of God", with
that oral jurisprudence that threw a protective hedge around it
by fixing the rules of conduct for every situation in life; in this
he sees a "human tradition" added to the Law of God which, in
practice, actually jeopardizes this Law of God (Mk. 7, 8-13). At
other times Jesus brings the Law itself to a fulfillment that goes
beyond the letter of the Law because its old formulation was
partly conditioned by the hardness of the human heart: "You
have heard that it was said . . . but I say to you. . . ." (Mt. 5,
21-48; cf. 19, 8). As he brings to man the kingdom of God, the
promised salvation, the grace that was expected, he is in a situation where he can promulgate that "law of freedom" (Jas. 1, 25),
the rule of which is the imitation of divine perfection (Mt. 5, 48),
and the heart of which is the commandment of love (Mt. 22, 34-
40). We can see in what sense Jesus *abrogated* what was merely
human tradition or mere divine accommodation to the weakness
of man (e.g., the possibility of divorce or the law of retaliation
explicitly written into the positive law of the Old Testament).
By doing this he not only substituted his teaching for the tradition
of the elders but even for the letter of the scriptures! Thus he
taught "with authority" and not like the scribes (Mk. 1, 22) who
always sought shelter behind the "chain of tradition" they had
inherited.[8]

However, in spite of this liberty with regard to the *halacha* of
the pharisees (cf. Mk. 2, 23; 3, 3-5. 15-17; 7, 1-5), Jesus fre-
quented the temple and obeyed its rites; he took part in the prayer
of the synagogue with its customary formulas as well as the
psalms; occasionally he made use of the *haggada* grafted on to
the interpretation of the scriptures, as at the feast of the Taber-

---

[8] Cf. E. Bikerman, La chaîne de la tradition pharisienne," in *Rev. Bibl.*
59 (1952), pp. 44-54.

nacles (Jn. 7, 37).[9] And so, he supports a fair amount of traditional elements in his practical conduct, but his attitude toward
them is the same as that toward the sacred texts: he *fulfills* them,
which means at the same time integration and going to the limit,
continuity and going beyond. In short, the *newness of the Gospel*
tied up with his person embraces the whole positive content of
scripture and tradition, but in a way which transforms them: in
him the whole meaning of Judaism changes.

2. *Jesus as the Source of a New Tradition*

In this way Jesus remolds everything he touches, and so becomes the source of a new tradition for those who believe in the
Gospel. If he does not write anything down, his Person, his words,
his deeds, his conduct, his way of praying to the Father, the events
which shape his human destiny and end in his death and resurrection—all these factors constitute at the same time an end and
a beginning. His life is a *revelation in actions* in which the whole
design of God in the past, the whole of the ancient scriptures and
all the values contained in Judaism were subjected to an astonishing transfiguration. Now, this eschatological manifestation of
the Word of God is not left to the uncertain hazards of human
witness. Jesus called those who witnessed his life and heard his
Word to a faith which is a docile response to God speaking within
(Jn. 6, 44-45). From among those who believed he chose his
messengers, whom he made his official witnesses (Acts 1, 8).
Even during his life he made them take the Gospel to places
where he could not go in person (Mt. 10). In this way he laid the
foundations of a new community that would preserve the tradition he inaugurated: the Church (Mt. 16, 18).

For these men, the Person of Jesus replaced all the authorities
that watched over the Jewish tradition with a particular interest
in its liturgical and juridical features: priests and doctors, whether
they were Sadducees, Pharisees or Essenes. In their eyes, Jesus
was the *one and only teacher* (Mt. 23, 8). On his part, in order

[9] Cf. *Rev. Bibl.* 66 (1959), pp. 369-74; 67 (1960), pp. 224-25; 70
(1963), pp. 43-51 (with reference to the most recent studies).

to train them for their mission, Jesus did not mind using the methods of oral tradition which were current among the learned men of that time and which fell in line with the prophets and the ancient teachers of wisdom. It is from within this framework that he finally sent them out to teach all nations so that men can learn to observe all that he has commanded them (cf. Mt. 28, 20). There is therefore nothing strange in the fact that the apostolic Church was a "guardian of traditions".

III

1. The Sacred Tradition of Jesus

The twelve "eyewitnesses and ministers of the Word" (Lk. 1, 2), who followed Jesus "from the baptism of John until the day when he was taken up from us" (Acts 1, 22), were the depositaries of an oral and concrete tradition whose substance they could not change since it was the sacred legacy left them by the Lord himself. In fact, the unbiased critical study of the gospels not only allows us to get behind the synthesis set out in these four small writings and into the original environment where their matter took shape; it also allows us to examine the mentality and preoccupations of that environment. Now, the structure of this environment, where the college of the Twelve exercised a normative authority, prevented the environment itself from creating an arbitrary expression of its beliefs. "All that Jesus began to do and teach, until the day when he was taken up, after he had given commandments through the Holy Spirit to the apostles whom he had chosen" (Acts 1, 1-2)—this was now imposed on everyone much more authoritatively than was the case with the opinions of the doctors in the rabbinical tradition.

This is not the place for a detailed inventory of the contents and forms of this basic information. If one wanted to do this, he would have to distinguish two elements: the *sayings* of Jesus, already fixed to a certain degree before the preaching of the apostles transmitted them to the people, and the *remembering of*

Jesus' deeds and facts about him, already engraved in their memory but not yet given a literary expression. In any case, when one tries to get a picture of the way in which this "sacred tradition of Jesus" [10] was transmitted, one should not think of a mechanically faithful reproduction and be concerned only with collecting exact phrases and details. This is rather a matter of a *living faithfulness* that presupposes two things at the same time: a profound understanding of the words and deeds of Jesus within the totality of his mystery and of the Christian experience that derives from it, and a practical adaptation to the needs and possibilities of the environment in which his Gospel was proclaimed. The apostles were given the Holy Spirit to ensure the first point (Acts 1, 8; Jn. 15, 26f.; 16, 13); the second was a matter of pastoral wisdom. All this leads us to the crucial issue of the apostolic tradition.

2. *The Apostolic Tradition*

The existence of the apostolic tradition can be approached from two sources that influence each other. First of all, the Acts of the Apostles stresses the part played in Jerusalem and Judea by the college of the Twelve whose leader is Peter. The members of the Christian community "devoted themselves to the apostles' teaching and fellowship, to the breaking of bread and the prayers" (Acts 2, 42), while "the apostles with great power gave their testimony to the resurrection of the Lord Jesus" (Acts 4, 33). We are therefore not confronted with groups of more or less anarchic illuminists who would work out the expression of their religious feeling as they pleased; such a view would be wholly gratuitous and run counter to all the texts. The Twelve not only exercise an unquestioned authority over the community of Jerusalem, but they also maintain an effective control over the Churches that are born of it: Peter and John undertake a mission in Samaria on that basis (Acts 8, 14); Barnabas is sent to Antioch to check up on the kind of gospel preached there and the communal life led there (Acts 11, 22).

[10] X. Léon-Dufour, *Les évangiles et l'histoire de Jésus* (Paris, 1963), pp. 293-315.

This picture of the situation, too general and too little detailed for my liking, corresponds exactly to the personal witness of the other source, St. Paul [11] who was so attached to his prerogative as an apostle through a personal "revelation of Jesus Christ" (Gal. 1, 1. 11f.). He bears witness to the existence of certain traditions of which he is simply the depositary. He explicitly mentions two of them in his first letter to the Corinthians: the tradition of the celebration of the Lord's supper, a liturgical action linked to a historical remembrance (11, 23ff.), and the tradition of Jesus' resurrection, not as an object of speculation but as a matter of witness (15, 3-7). In both cases it is symptomatic that Paul takes over the technical vocabulary of the rabbinical tradition which he knows from experience in order to show what he has *received* and what he in his turn *transmits*. Some other allusions (as in 1 Cor. 7, 10-11) corroborate this and show how he depends on a basic tradition he had to receive when he entered the Church, either at Damascus (Acts 9, 17-18) or at Jerusalem when he visited Peter "after three years" (Gal. 1, 18).

Can we state a little more precisely the contents of this tradition of the Twelve to which the personal testimony of Paul adds some precision but which he does not contradict in substance? It includes, first of all, what has been called above the "sacred tradition of Jesus". But this is not simply a subject to be preached in order to prompt individual conversions, after which the believers would organize themselves as they thought fit. The proclamation of the Gospel cannot be separated from the institution in charge of it, the Church, where the believers meet in order to live, pray and act together under the direction of those who represent Christ himself. The communion of the Holy Spirit lies at the very heart of what the apostles *hand down* to the people (Acts 2, 38). This is done jointly by two means: the reception of the Gospel which is "the power of God for salvation", and the practical participation in actions which express the life of the

[11] L. Cerfaux, "La tradition selon saint Paul; Les deux points de départ de la tradition chrétienne," in *Recueil L. Cerfaux,* Vol. II, pp. 253-82; B. Rigaux, "De traditione apud S. Paulum," in *De Scriptura et Traditione,* ed. C. Balić (Rome, 1963), pp. 137-69.

Church. Baptism, imposition of hands, celebration of the Lord's supper, explanation of the scriptures, transmission of a teaching which regulates Christian moral conduct—all this is an integral part of the apostolic tradition. It follows *a fortiori* that the structures representing the authority of the apostles in all these communities cannot be separated from this tradition, for it is because of these structures that the apostolic tradition is secured against the hazards of social and ideological evolution to which these communities would otherwise be subject. It constitutes the *depositum*[12] with which the envoys of the apostles and those responsible for the local Churches are entrusted. On this point the pastoral epistles (1 Tim. 6, 20; 2 Tim. 1, 12f.; 2, 2; 3, 14; Tit. 2, 1) and Paul's discourse to the elders of Ephesus are clear.

Thus, even during the lifetime of the apostles, the *apostolic tradition* which shaped the Gospel and the Church passed into the *ecclesiastical tradition,* spread out over the various ministries which must "guard what has been entrusted to them" (1 Tim. 6, 20). This, in fact, covers every aspect of the Church's life: proclamation of the Gospel, apologetics, prayer and liturgy, the Christian *halacha,* the thinking about the scriptures (i.e., the Old Testament), and so on. In this structure one no doubt finds elements of the Jewish tradition, but they have been sifted and reinterpreted. There is no need to suppose that there was an authoritative intervention by the Twelve or by Paul, or that there was a plenary consultation, of the kind reported in Acts 15 (cf. Gal. 2, 1-10), at the beginning of every development that this apostolic tradition may have experienced in the course of the 1st century. It is sufficient that a profound sense of unity in faith and a conscious acceptance of the teaching of the apostles (Acts 2, 42) insured among all those that took part in it a genuine communion of thought where the apostolic deposit remained the basic element. Because of this the responsible ministers appointed by Paul and the Twelve or by their envoys and successors have an essential function to perform, as for example, Barnabas at

---

[12] C. Spicq, *Les épîtres pastorales* (Études bibliques) (Paris, 1947), pp. 327-35.

Antioch (Acts 11, 22-26; 13, 1). With this point established we can now proceed to see how the books of the New Testament originated.

3. *The Birth of the New Testament*

Like the community of Israel, the Church of the apostolic age possessed a functional literature adapted to its needs, structures, cultural level and practical opportunities. To start with, this literature incorporated from the beginning the literature of the Old Testament which the Church had received from the Jewish synagogue, in Hebrew in Judaea, in the Greek of the Jews of Alexandria, in the diaspora. The use of these books as the Word of God determined the *canon of the scriptures* for the Church, and this required no legal decision. The list fixed among the Jews of Palestine toward 90 A.D., when this Judaism was reorganized under the direction of the pharisaic school of Hillel, would have been too late to be authoritative on this point. The use of the Old Testament was naturally accompanied by a normative interpretation which would put these texts in the perspective of Christ. On all this, however, we have unfortunately only fragmentary information in the New Testament. But it would be methodically wrong to try to reconstruct the apostolic tradition by taking only these fragments as a basis, because in the ecclesiastical tradition of the two following centuries the establishment of the canon aimed only at preserving apostolic usage.[13] But this use of the Jewish bible—which had now become the Christian bible— could not suffice for the needs of the Church. On the other hand, the existence of its oral and practical tradition in no way ruled out the need for texts that were fixed and preserved in writing at a time when the written word played an important part in the Church's environment, whether Jewish or Hellenistic. This is the reason why the documents of the New Testament came into existence.

Insofar as the evangelical tradition is concerned, we must take into consideration a period of oral transmission during which the

[13] Cf. my explanation in *La Bible, Parole de Dieu, op. cit.,* pp. 144-51.

material collected in our four gospels took shape, in the case of some episodes very briefly (as with the narrative of the Last Supper in 1 Cor. 11, 23ff.), in case of others at much greater length (as with the narrative of the childhood of Jesus or the discourses in John). This point is never lost sight of in Catholic exegesis which has even occasionally tended to overestimate the importance of this indiscriminate oral tradition at the expense of the direct literary interdependence between the various collections of the gospels.

From a different point of view the same point has been emphasized for the last ten years by several Scandinavian scholars whose colleagues applied the method of "criticism of the traditions" to the Old Testament, as we have seen. Older studies by V. Taylor and C. H. Dodd surely paved the way for them.[14] But at the Congress of Oxford in 1957, H. Riesenfeld launched a sort of manifesto on this point:[15] reacting against the hypothesis of the "creative community" too easily accepted by critical scholars at the beginning of the century and by certain upholders of the *Formgeschichte,* he showed that the real environment that gave birth to the gospels was the apostolic tradition.

During the years that followed B. Gerhardsson contrasted, in a penetrating study, "the oral tradition and the written transmission in rabbinical Judaism and primitive Christianity".[16] According to him Palestinian Christianity borrowed the necessary technique for the oral transmission of the materials that constitute the Gospel tradition from rabbinism. The critical study of the synoptic texts must therefore take into account the laws that are peculiar to that oral tradition which must be postulated before the composition of the written collections. This point of view would fit in well with that of an older work by K. Stendahl who sought the

[14] V. Taylor, *The Formation of the Gospel Tradition* (London, 1933); C. H. Dodd, *The Apostolic Preaching and Its Development* (London, 1934).

[15] H. Riesenfeld, *The Gospel Tradition and Its Beginnings* (London, 1937) (=*Studia Evangelica*, Texte und Untersuch. 73 [Berlin, 1959], pp. 43-65).

[16] B. Gerhardsson, *Memory and Manuscript* (Uppsala, 1961).

origin of St. Matthew's gospel in a school of Christian teachers.[17] On another point I may mention that contemporary studies devoted to the fourth gospel are inclined to favor the hypothesis of an oral Johannine tradition which may have prepared, stage by stage, the final synthesis that appeared at the end of the 1st century.

All these studies point to a problem of methodology which is, in fact, very important. Neither the synoptic question nor that of St. John's gospel can be solved by the sole use of classical literary criticism as was formerly implied in the so-called theory of "the two sources", or as it was recently used by L. Vaganay in his book on the synoptic problem.[18] But here again we should beware of a certain extremism. First of all, the oral tradition should not be thought of as a simple mechanical transmission of the *ipsissima verba Jesu,* the very same words that Jesus used, in the way in which M. Jousse suggested that the gospels were recited and memorized;[19] if there are such recitative pieces, their literary formation may take place at any level of tradition and the problem of their composition would demand a new study in each particular case. Indeed, the way in which the apostles and Christian teachers shaped the basic material was always intent on adjusting this deposit, which is normative for the faith, to the practical use for which all the texts were destined. The historical criticism of literary form and editing therefore have their place in discovering the relation between the writings and the concrete life of the communities for which they were written.

The problem of the literary *genre* of each gospel is linked up with the twofold relation of the pericopes and final compositions with the living tradition of the Church. On the one hand there is their dependence on the apostolic tradition from which they derive their substance; on the other there is their adaptation to the ecclesiastical tradition as it is alive in the environment where re-

---

[17] K. Stendahl, *The School of St. Matthew* (Uppsala, 1954).

[18] L. Vaganay, *Le problème synoptique* (Tournai-Paris, 1954).

[19] M. Jousse, *Le style oral et mnémotechnique chez les verbo-moteurs* (Paris, 1925); used by L. de Grandmaison in *Jésus Christ,* Vol. I (Paris, 1928), pp. 201-09.

sponsible authors are busy with the editing of the texts. Their literary structure, their explicit or implicit theology, their literary conventions—all are determined by this last point. In this perspective the question about the literary editors is rather secondary because it is not necessary for the gospels to have been edited by the apostles themselves in order to represent the apostolic tradition in an authentic manner. It is enough that the final editors used material taken from the apostolic deposit, even though they adapted it to the practical requirements of their environment and their age, and that they were intent, even in their way of adapting the matter, on being faithful to the deposit as they used it. There is no difficulty in granting this point for Mark and Luke, but there is no reason why we should not grant it also for the canonical texts of Matthew and John.

But it is not only the gospels in the strict sense with which we are concerned here. Luke added to his work a presentation of the Gospel in history (the Acts of the Apostles) which is partly based on the oral tradition of Christianity in Palestine. Moreover, apart from the Pauline epistles which are unquestionably authentic, there developed an epistolary literature, whose origin is much less clear. Now, regardless of the question of dates and authors, these writings have one essential feature in common: they are *pastoral documents* written to fill the concrete requirements of a given Church or group of Churches. In many cases their text reflects certain practical features of the Church's life in detail: liturgy, preaching, explanation of the scriptures, etc. The way in which these details are rooted in the living tradition shows again the need for an intelligent *Formgeschichte,* which can throw light on their literary structure and their bearing, while at the same time enriching our knowledge of primitive Christianity.

There remains the question of authorship. To solve it we must beware of two ways of oversimplifying the matter. One way is to start from a traditional attribution and to understand by "author" what we mean today by that term in literature. The other way would be to attribute spurious texts, about which the 2nd-century Church would have been curiously mistaken, to forgers who would be solely concerned with spreading their own ideas. In fact, all these texts mean to preserve the genuine apostolic tradition—whether Pauline, Petrine, Johannine or other—in a form and according to literary conventions which have to be specified in each case. This is true not only of the epistles to which the critics like to attribute some "intermediate" authenticity (e.g., the epistle to the Ephesians or the first epistle of St. Peter). If we can read, it holds just as much for those that create most complex literary problems: the pastoral epistles which concentrate on the preservation of the "deposit" entrusted by Paul to the leaders of the Churches; the epistle of Jude and the second epistle of Peter which combat the false teachers that try to pervert the apostolic teaching; finally, the first epistle of St. John which reacts against the anti-Christs, enemies of the Faith.

In short, in whatever way the apostolic tradition was crystallized in one or another particular document, even by means of a spurious attribution (as in the second epistle of Peter), the content and composition of the text is rooted in an utter attachment to that tradition which the Churches must guard faithfully in order to live by it. The second epistle of Peter even shows us how—in an ecclesiastical tradition where the memory of the apostles is kept alive—people were anxious not only to get to know their oral or practical inheritance but also to gather the writings that come down from the apostles. Apart from the first epistle of Peter (3, 1) the author indeed knows a collection of Pauline epistles which he ranks with the "other scriptures", that is, the Old Testament (3, 15-16). Thus the process of assembling a canon of texts started even before the New Testament drew to a close. Nevertheless, we have to wait until the 2nd century for a complete collection of writings that are authoritative because they directly represent the apostolic tradition. This last fact shows that the oldest ecclesiastical tradition, while conscious of "guarding the deposit" with the help of its various ministries, nevertheless sought to test its own veracity by using these writings as a touchstone. These were no doubt occasional writings, limited in subject and in explicit witness to doctrine, but they were intimately bound up with the pastoral life of a Church where the apostolic tradition could still be grasped as the source of that life.

Therefore, we see the fact of tradition did not begin with Christ or with the subapostolic Church, but rather with the beginnings of Israel. In this framework two elements came to the fore in history which gave birth to both the Jewish and the Christian faith: the sign-events, in which the people could recognize God's deeds, and the Word of God. The data of revelation and the life it brought to mankind were always preserved, primarily by means of a living tradition that embraced the whole existence of the People of God and its social structures. The change brought about by Christ did not affect the general conditions of the problem on this point, although the witness of the apostles put an end to further revelation. Yet, in both Testaments, the divine Word brought by the prophets (in the broad sense) and the apostles was not solely entrusted to the responsibility of the community, even a community assisted by the Spirit of God. God has willed that his Word be also crystallized in texts in which the living tradition took shape at a level which would enable it to serve as a norm for the further development of tradition. Two points should be dealt with in greater detail: (1) the process in which the text came to be established, of which both Testaments contain numerous examples; (2) the method to be used in order to recover from these texts the fullness of the divine Word by which the Church continues to live. However, these points would go beyond the scope of this article.

Joseph Schreiner/*Münster, W. Germany*

The Development
of the Israelite "Credo"

If the people of the old covenant is asked about the content of its faith, the answer comes in the form of narratives and reports. Not, of course, that theoretical statements about the nature of God, the order of the world, human existence and the conduct of life are lacking. The wisdom of the ancient East might have stimulated such reflections arising from man's great questions about the meaning and fulfillment of existence; nevertheless, Israel's thinking from its very origin was otherwise oriented. There was no question of building up out of pure meditation a systematic understanding of the self and the world or presenting in myth an explanation of the properties of being. Israel was filled with the experiences that had befallen it from God. This experience had to be expressed; this insight had to be grasped in mental forms.

The fact that Israel did this is proved by the scriptures it left behind as the testimony of its faith. For the most part these speak in the form of reports about God, man and the world, in a way suited to the people's faith-experience of Yahweh. With few exceptions, they are historical books or works that give information about events. Even the writings of the prophets and most of the psalms are of this kind. They deal with events that have already taken place or with such as will occur in the future. We may certainly say that in Israel's scriptures we are presented with a description of what is happening. History is undoubtedly its main topic.[1]

This special character of the Old Testament is the logical outcome of the process in which God made himself known. The Old Testament people of the covenant experienced its God in history. Divine revelation did not come to it in the form of doctrinal statements that were then merely to be accepted, preserved and developed. Yahweh let himself be perceived in his works. In his action he revealed his nature and his will. Even when he delivered his message by word, it was in order to operate in the world and on man. Every word of God possessed efficacious power and the character of a deed; it was properly, fundamentally and essentially a divine action. Yahweh revealed himself to his people as the living God, active in word and deed. If Israel—as was intended in the plan of the Lord—was to put God's revelation into human words, this was scarcely possible other than by representing and copying down this divine operation in the reflection of faith.[2]

If the people of the covenant wanted to confess its allegiance to Yahweh, it was simply compelled to celebrate his saving action. If it wished to give an account of its faith, it had to speak pertinently and appropriately, in acknowledgment and assent, of the divine saving deeds and of the God behind them. Israel spoke of God's deeds and thereby confessed: "This is God, our God. . . . He will be our guide forever" (Ps. 48, 15). The entire ancient tradition of the people of Yahweh, as recorded in the Pentateuch, is a wide ranging song of praise of the divine action. But in early times, too, the People of God had already tried to capture in concise statements what Yahweh had done to it or for it.

[1] L. Köhler, *Theologie des Alten Testaments* (Tübingen, ³1953), p. 77; cf. Eng. tr.: *Old Testament Theology* (Philadelphia, 1958).
[2] "With thought and speech oriented to salvation history, Israel took up and formulated by far the greater part of Old Testament revelation": J. Schreiner, "Führung—Thema der Heilsgeschichte im Alten Testament," in *Bibl. Zeitschrift* 5 (1961), pp. 2-18, esp. p. 3.

1. *Ancient Formulas Imprinted with Israel's Experience of Faith*

One of the oldest formulations used in Israel's confession of faith is the statement: "Yahweh brought us out of Egypt." This and similar forms are found throughout the Old Testament. This expression already exists almost as a formula and as the indispensable quotation of a fundamental truth in the ancient pronouncements of Balaam (Num. 23, 22; 24, 8) and at the beginning of the decalogue (Exod. 20, 2; Deut. 5, 6). This statement probably emerged out of the immediate experience in the hour of deliverance, whether coined by the people involved or proclaimed as an interpretation of the event by Moses.

This proclamation, praising the redeeming intervention of the Lord, became Israel's primal confession.[3] No other event and no later manifestation of divine glory and divine will could displace this article of faith. Neither the gift of the covenant embracing all salvation nor the gift of God's presence in the sanctuary gained a greater importance in the statements of faith. Even Jeroboam I found himself compelled to fall back on this statement about the liberation from Egyptian bondage (1 Kg. 12, 28) when he set up shrines of the kingdom in Dan and Bethel. Could Yahweh be honored without confessing his saving deed at the Red Sea?

Not much younger is that other formula in which Israel with the utmost conciseness expressed its relationship to God: "Yahweh is our God!" These words ring out innumerable times in the Old Testament texts or are reechoed in them. They sum up all that took place between Israel and Yahweh. In particular, election and covenant are included. The judgment is by no means excluded, but the stress is laid on the divine grant of salvation for the Lord had taken this people to himself to do good to it in kindness and fidelity. Properly speaking—one might think—the phrase, "Yahweh is our God", ought to suffice as a completely

[3] Cf. M. Noth, *Überlieferungsgeschichte des Pentateuch* (Darmstadt, [2]1960), p. 52.

valid confession of faith, for it expresses in the most profound and straightforward way what Israel could say to God. Furthermore, as a recoining in the form of a confession of the covenant formula, "I am your God; you are my people", it recalls the fundamental datum of the covenant with God which embraces the whole man together with his thinking and willing. What more could he do than to put into this confession his whole trust and his whole devotion?

However, if the people of Yahweh wanted to sing the praises of its God, this basic word acknowledgment of the covenant reality was not enough; Israel had to express, at least in broad outline, what he had done. Soon fixed expressions emerged, containing what was essential for the vision of faith. Israel spoke of the "beautiful and spacious land the Lord had given". Ancient tradition could report that Yahweh had already "sworn to the fathers that he would give this land". It was aware too that "Abraham, Isaac and Jacob" had wandered about "as strangers in Canaan". But the "God of the fathers made them become numerous" after they had "descended into Egypt".[4]

God's people constantly spoke of the basic facts of salvation history. In this way all those who confessed and listened were reminded of the content implied in the formula, "our God". Its existential import became visible and its closeness to life perceptible.

But the name of Yahweh also had to be brought home to the experience of the believer, who naturally asked: "Who then is this God who was revealed in his saving action and whom I worship?" Israel, in its consciousness of faith, did not neglect this task. Affirmations of God from the Canaanite environment came to its aid. So far as it was possible to translate these and fill them with the content of Israelite faith, they were taken over. Ancient formulations thus came to be used with a new sound: Yahweh

---

[4] On the theme of the promised land, cf. G. von Rad, "Verheissenes Land und Jahwes Land im Hexateuch," in *Gesammelte Studien zum Alten Testament* (Munich, 1958), pp. 87-100.

and no other is the "living God" and "supreme God, creator of heaven and earth".[5] Yahweh—not an incomprehensible El or a localized Baal—"is king" (Pss. 93, 1: 97, 1).

If with the primal confession and the basic word of the covenant there was linked an allegiance to the worship of Yahweh alone, so the appropriation of foreign ideas and their conversion into Israelite formulas of faith necessarily carried with it a more determined rejection of other gods. If these formulas were elevated to the status of a confession, there lay in them a denial of strange divinities.[6] This development was of great importance for the formation of the ideas of Israelite faith. It made no slight contribution to the fact that God's people was finally able to profess a clear and intact monotheism.

For Israel, however, Yahweh's identity had to be discovered first and foremost in his wondrous deeds. In this respect, too, the people of the Lord succeeded in recapturing in concise statements the insights they had been given. To quote but one of these, consider the article of faith which Israelite tradition considered so important and characteristic that it incorporated it into the account of God's appearance on Sinai: "The Lord, the Lord, a God merciful and gracious, slow to anger and abounding in steadfast love and faithfulness, keeping steadfast love for thousands, forgiving iniquity and transgression and sin, but who will by no means clear the guilty" (Exod. 34, 6-7).

Thus the People of God of the old covenant—as can be shown with just a few essential examples—formulated statements to give expression to its faith. The question arises as to what compelled it to form such declarations of faith and what situation made this possible.

[5] On these titles, cf. L. Köhler, op. cit., pp. 36, 39f; T. C. Vriezen, Theologie des Alten Testaments in Grundzugen (Neukirchen), pp. 141-47, 155-64; cf. Eng. tr.: Outline of Old Testament Theology (Newton Centre, Mass.).

[6] C. Westermann, "Bekenntnis im AT und im Judentum," in Die Religion in Geschichte und Gegenwart I, pp. 988ff., mentions among the features of the confession that "it has the character of decision".

2. The Cultic "Sitz im Leben"

Undoubtedly the above mentioned statements of faith do not emerge from the sphere of private devotion because in their very origins they are too much permeated by the reference to the whole people and they bear too obviously the characteristics of the hymnal style of the great cultic celebration. We have only to open the book of Psalms to come across the source from which the Old Testament formulas of faith have sprung. It is the worship of the people of Yahweh, the covenant celebration of the community that the Lord has chosen for himself. Here Israel spoke of the foundations of its existence and sang the praises of its God. In all this it could not fail to recall the divine saving deeds, for it was through these that the people of the Lord had been created. This recollection was required by the so-called covenant formula (cf. Jos. 24, 2-13),[7] which the people of the twelve tribes, with a true sense of the basic structure and basic facts of its existence, had appropriated to itself so that it might represent with this schema the covenant with God.

In this formulary God introduces himself and immediately afterward the prehistory of the covenant is expounded. The mention of Yahweh's saving deeds, therefore, could not be omitted from the celebrations of Israelite feasts at which the association with God was lauded. Consequently, "the recognition, confession and recollection of the great deeds of Yahweh are both a serious concern of faith and a pious duty".[8] It is a law in Israel that the tribes should praise his name in this way (Ps. 122, 4). Thus they respond to the vocation which has been granted to them (cf. Ps. 147, 7).

The ancient tradition also knows of such an obligation of a confession of faith before the whole community. In response to the divine deed of redemption at the Red Sea, Miriam sings before all the people the briefest and certainly the oldest hymn of the Old Testament:

[7] Cf. K. Baltzer, "Das Bundesformular," in *Wissenschaftliche Monographien zum Alten und Neuen Testament* 4 (Neukirchen, 1960).

[8] A. Weiser, "Die Psalmen," in *Das Alte Testament Deutsch* 14/15 (Göttingen, ⁵1959), p. 50.

Sing to the Lord, for he has triumphed gloriously;
the horse and his rider he has thrown into the sea.

(Exod. 15, 21)

At all times the People of God praised the wondrous works of
the Lord which they had experienced. In this constant praise were
formed the statements of faith which it regarded as its confession
to God.

With the entry into Canaan, Israel's horizon was also extended
in a theological sense. Under the influence of forms of worship
and hymns used at the Canaanite shrines, Israel began to per-
ceive a deed of God that had been scarcely or little noticed in
the desert period. This is the work of creation in all its aspects
of divine world dominion and world conservation. An abundance
of words of praise, glorifying Yahweh as creator of heaven and
earth and singing of his power over the whole world, gained en-
trance into all forms of Israel's prayer. They developed into set
phrases suitable for expressing the consciousness of faith. Nevertheless, from a historical standpoint these formularies were of
secondary importance. In the vision of faith of Yahweh's people
it was always the events of saving history which came to the fore,
even when praise of God the creator and his attributes came to
occupy a large space in cultic songs.

However, we must not overlook the fact that cult, which pre-
serves all traditions, is simultaneously their living realization.
This held true also for the Israelite act of worship. It compelled
the people to find for the present moment new expressions of the
abiding reality. Thus new formulas were added and the old were
equipped with special stresses. Israel's articles of faith were never
formulated as finished and ready-made. During the Old Testament period the Israelite credo did not acquire a final formulation
in words. It was always possible to say some things differently
and to take in new elements, for God also acted and revealed himself after the occupation of the promised land and continued to
do so in salvation history. It was therefore in connection with
the cultic *Sitz im Leben* that the Israelite confession of faith was

formed, but it did not gain a final expression in words. Its basic structure did however take on a firm shape, and this probably existed in early times. Its essential characteristics can be perceived in various Old Testament texts.

3. The "Minor Historical Credo" [9]

In Deuteronomy we find the following cultic text:

A wandering Aramean was my father; and he went down into Egypt and sojourned there, few in number; and there he became a nation, great, mighty and populous. And the Egyptians treated us harshly, and afflicted us, and laid upon us hard bondage. Then we cried to the Lord, the God of our fathers, and the Lord heard our voice and saw our affliction, our toil and our oppression. And the Lord brought us out of Egypt with a mighty hand and an outstretched arm, with great terror, with signs and wonders, and he brought us into this place and gave us this land, a land flowing with milk and honey.   (Deut. 26, 5-9)

These words are not a prayer but a confession, "presumably the oldest that we can discover".[10] It is only the following sentence that turns the whole into a prayer of thanksgiving: "And behold, now I bring the first of the fruit of the ground, which thou, O Lord, hast given me" (Deut. 26, 10).

One from among the people solemnly confesses God's deeds in salvation history. Through his mouth the whole assembled community speaks. Only at one point does he make a personal confession: at the beginning, when he says "my father" and not— as the rest of the confession might lead us to expect—"our father". The father here is Jacob. This reference of the speaker to himself is required by the occasion on which he makes his

[9] The designation is that of G. von Rad, "Das formgeschichtliche Problem des Hexateuch," in *Gesammelte Studien zum Alten Testament* (Munich, 1958), pp. 9-86.
[10] *Ibid.*, pp. 12f.

confession.[11] He has come to the shrine to confirm to Yahweh, his God, that he has reached the land which the Lord promised by oath to the fathers (v. 3). Therefore, he incorporates in the credo his own personal relationship to the fathers of Israel. In this connection he may have recalled the prayer of Jacob who confessed to the God of his fathers, Abraham and Isaac, when he had returned into the land of Canaan: "With only my staff I crossed this Jordan; and now I have become two companies" (Gen. 32, 10). From unpretentious beginnings and an unpromising situation the Lord had brought him to prosperity in the possession of the promised land, a prelude to that salvation history which God's people and this Israelite making his thanksgiving had experienced.

In celebrating this gift of salvation in the minor credo, Israel followed its historical course: from the time when the fathers were strangers in Canaan, by way of the Egyptian bondage, Yahweh's liberation of the people and his leading of them through the desert, up to the grant of the promised land. Almost the whole Pentateuch—of course, in the utmost brevity—is contained in this confession. But it is striking that the covenant on Sinai is absent,[12] not being mentioned even in a single word. Still more striking is the absence of the Sinai event in the instruction of Deuteronomy 6, 20-24. The father answers his son's question about the meaning of the Law with the schema of salvation history in the form of a confession, but without recalling the revelation of the Law at the mountain of God in the desert. This fact forces us to the conclusion that at the time of Deuteronomy the confession of salvation history had acquired a fixed and apparently unchangeable structure in which the covenant at Sinai was not mentioned.

The explanation of this state of affairs is provided by the

[11] This is pointed out by L. Rost, "Das kleine geschichtliche Credo," in *Das kleine Credo und andere Studien zum Alten Testament* (Heidelberg, 1965), pp. 11-25.

[12] G. von Rad emphasizes this and draws the conclusion that the Sinai tradition and that of the occupation of the land emerged independently of each other in different groups of traditions (*op. cit.*, pp. 13f.).

covenant formulary of Joshua 24. Here too, in Joshua's speech, the presentation of salvation history follows the form of the minor credo. Although it is considerably enlarged here by various individual traits, there is lacking any sort of account of the meeting with God on Sinai. Probably it is intentionally omitted. The reason for this might have been that in Sichem the covenant with Yahweh was made again or freshly contracted by the tribes who arrived later (v. 25). The participants, however, were not to appeal as disinterested parties to a distant, past event, but were to be accepted here and now existentially into the covenant association. Thus Israel received it in every generation: "Not with our fathers did the Lord make this covenant, but with us who are all of us here alive this day" (Deut. 5, 3). The reason why the profession of faith, drawn and worked out from the covenant formulary by the people of Yahweh in its early period,[13] contains no word about the covenant on Sinai is in order that God's saving deeds should be linked on the spot with the living, and that the existing community might be incorporated inescapably into God's covenant.

4. Development in Prayer and Preaching

The Israelite credo was not a dead possession. Growing out of worship, it was brought to life in the cultic celebration. It was unfolded in instructions and songs of praise. The so-called historical psalms furnish evidence of this development. The thanksgiving liturgy in the form of a litany (Ps. 136), in enumerating the historical saving deeds of God, follows the schema of the ancient confession (vv. 10-22). But it takes an important step further by incorporating the divine deed of creation (vv. 4-9). The confession praises first God the creator and then the Lord of salvation history. The emphasis is placed on the great historical deeds of Yahweh, while in Psalm 135 these fall back so that the emphasis is on the rejection of the idols of the nations (v. 15).

[13] The same schema is also attested to by Hosea 12, 13f.; 1 Samuel 12, 6ff.; Genesis 15, 13-15.

Psalm 78 gives ample space to the themes of the credo. Twice (vv. 12-29 and 42-55) the singer develops these with many details. Above all, he carefully describes the wondrous works in the desert, which became a temptation for the people, and the Egyptian plagues, which were a punishment for obstinacy. Here his concern becomes perceptible. The representation of salvation history in the form of a confession acquires the dark background of divine judgment and is meant to warn against apostasy and obduracy.

After mentioning the exile, the psalmist takes the themes of the confession further, up to the election of David and Sion (vv. 68-70). The psalm of salvation history in Exodus 15, 1-18 also closes with a mention of the temple of Sion.

In the long run, these extensions cannot be connected with the original schema. On the other hand, in Psalm 105—which recalls particularly the history of the fathers and the Egyptian plagues— the covenant theme (vv. 8-10) makes its way into the confession. The occupation of the land is here understood as the redemption of the covenant promise; Sinai, however, is not mentioned. The entire period of exile was able to make real the content of the ancient credo in such a way that it drew this into the prayer of petition (Ps. 106); in spite of the people's shameful ingratitude for God's saving deeds—shown by its sin and obstinacy—he did not wholly withdraw his favor. Therefore, may he likewise take pity, because of his covenant, on the community which recognizes and repents of its faults; may he help it again and grant it salvation! The groundwork of salvation history is depicted in this psalm in the form of a presentation of human delinquency and divine judgment. The prophet Ezekiel goes a step further. He makes use of the ancient confession (Ezek. 20) as a text for his sermon on punishment and judgment in order to outline a terrible history of disaster which Israel has itself incurred.

The penitential prayer of Nehemiah 9 marks a kind of final stage in the development of the Israelite credo. The tradition of salvation history which has evolved through the psalms mentioned above[14] is incorporated in this confession of sin. The confession of God the creator, the covenant of Sinai, the Law and God's judgment, the saving gifts of prophecy and kingship—all are introduced from the narrative in the Pentateuch into the ancient schema, considerably enlarged. The whole becomes a cry of repentance and petition, but at the same time it is praise of God (v. 5). The confession of faith always had to be the praise of God. Israel knew no other way.

Finally, it must be said that the whole Pentateuch, in the last analysis, is a wide-ranging enlargement of the ancient credo. It is not as if the people of Yahweh had been compelled to invent narratives and bring them in by force in order to fill out the skeleton of the themes (patriarchs—leading out—wandering in the desert—covenant—gift of the land) with historical life! The themes of the confession, corresponding to Israel's experience, merely show the narrators the way.

Conclusion

The Israelite credo in the Old Testament does not involve the whole content of the faith of Yahweh's people. It is open to the inclusion of new, divine, saving deeds. As we find it in the covenant celebration, it confesses God showing in his works his will to save; later it also confesses the creator and perhaps the judge. It was alive in cult and influential in prayer and preaching. But to the People of God of the new covenant it was able to give material and stimuli for the new confession.

[14] Psalms 105, 106 and 136 were used in the liturgy of the post-exilic community, as Chronicles testifies (1 Chr. 16; 2 Chr. 7, 3).

Joseph Blenkinsopp, S.D.B./ *Oxford, England*

Scope and Depth of Exodus Tradition in Deutero-Isaiah 40–55

I

THE EXODUS TRADITION

The exodus from Egypt was the founding experience of a group of tribes; it was the nucleus around which Israel was built. Historical Israel did not trace its beginnings back into the mists of the prehistoric past nor authenticate itself by reference to archetypal, mythological happenings as was the case with other peoples. The founding event took place in an historical epoch—the 13th century B.C. and the 19th Egyptian dynasty—which can to some extent be documented, and is expressed in terms drawn from the sociological and political realities of that time, such as the transference of political allegiance and land tenure: "We were pharaoh's slaves in Egypt . . . Yahweh redeemed us from Egypt . . . he gave us the land." This now stands out much more clearly with our increased knowledge of treaty-making, the protocol of international relations and the appeal to history in support of international treaty agreements in the ancient Near East.[1]

Another effect of this better understanding of the political dimension of early Israel's faith is that scholars are less inclined to accept the historical separation between covenant-traditions

---

[1] Cf. G. Mendenhall, *Law and Covenant in Israel and in the Ancient Near East* (Pittsburgh, 1955); J. Muilenburg, "Convenantal Formulations," in *Vetus Testamentum* 1 (1959), pp. 347ff.; K. Baltzer, *Das Bundesformular* (Neukirchen, 1960); D. J. McCarthy, *Treaty and Covenant* (Analecta Biblica) (Rome, 1963).

and exodus-tradition proposed by von Rad,[2] a point that will be relevant for our reading of Second Isaiah. The founding event begins with a community in an intolerable economic and political situation and deals in the first place with their economic and political salvation—"Yahweh brought them out from there." This remains a real dimension of the biblical revelation precisely because man's historical existence is taken seriously, providing no justification for an illegitimate extrapolation to another world, even when the events are symbolized.

The exodus is seen in the tradition as more than a once-for-all event. It came to have paradigmatic value as revealing the essential lines, the structure, of God's saving activity. Israel's was not *any* god, but he who "brought you out of the land of Egypt, out of the house of bondage" (Exod. 20, 2; Deut. 5, 6). It is here that we find the link between exodus and covenant, since this declaration of identity stands at the head of the covenant-law. The deuteronomic historian generally represents other groups which come into contact or collision with Israel as acknowledging this, such as the Gibeonites (Jos. 9, 9), and Philistines (1 Sam. 4, 8). Egyptian exodus universalized as transition from slavery to freedom, death to life, came to dominate Hebrew thinking about their God, and other groups which entered the covenant did so only when they saw the relevance for themselves of this pattern, even though they had not themselves been brought out of Egypt. As Mendenhall puts it: "The symbolization of historical events was possible because each group that entered the covenant could and did see the analogy between bondage and exodus and their own experience." [3] It is within this context of a gradual growth of theology and symbol around the primitive tradition that we have to situate the exodus passages in Second Isaiah.

What was the vehicle of this growth and development in the tradition? Tradition was in the first place a family affair, as is

[2] For a thorough examination and trenchant criticism of von Rad, together with essential bibliography, cf. A. Weiser, *Introduction to the Old Testament* (London, 1961), pp. 83-95.
[3] Cf. "The Hebrew Conquest of Palestine," in *Bibl. Archaeologist* 25. 3 (1962), p. 74.

clear from the fixed form of words used in the passover *haggada:*
"When your son asks you in time to come . . . you shall say to
your son"—and the passover was an exclusively family or clan
festival until about the time of Josiah.[4]

Anamnesis was of course a prominent feature of liturgical action as is clear from the formulaic recital made at the harvest
festival and numerous indications in the cultic hymns of Israel.[5]
But the exodus-theme is deployed also in the prophetic books
independently of the passover which is not mentioned in any pre-
exilic prophetic book. So, for example, in the *improperia* of
Amos and Micah, Yahweh identifies himself as the exodus-God
(Amos 2, 10; 3, 1-2; Mic. 6, 3). For Hosea Yahweh is "the Lord
your God from the land of Egypt" (12, 9; 13, 4) and, by com-
paring the menacing power of Assyria with that of Egypt 400
years before, he holds out for Israel the grim prospect of a return
to slavery. Exodus from Egypt and *eisodos* into the land are
thematic in Deuteronomy, the last recension of which dates from
the exilic period.

II

THE EXILE AS CRISIS OF FAITH

In itself the deportation of 586 B.C. was not an epoch-making
event except of course for those who took part in it. Such depor-
tations had been the order of the day since the period of Assyrian
expansion. It was not long before those exiles who had felt un-
able to take Jeremiah's advice to settle down in their new environment (Jer. 29, 5-9) could detect signs of an eventual release—
perhaps as early as the accession of Nabonidus (555) or at least
the release of the captive Jehoiachin (561). For the anonymous
prophet of Isaiah 40—55 the sign was the victorious career of
Cyrus the Persian, and most of the material in these chapters can
be dated confidently between his annexation of Lydia in 546 and
the fall of Babylon in October, 539. Addressing himself to those

[4] For the history of the passover, cf. H.-J. Kraus, *Gottesdienst in Israel*
(Munich, 1962), pp. 61-72; R. de Vaux, *Ancient Israel, Its Life and
Institutions* (London, 1961), pp. 484-93.
[5] Deut. 26, 1-11; Pss. 78; 105; 106.

exiles who had not been absorbed by their environment and who had retained their attachment to the Davidic dynasty and the national sense of destiny, he set himself to solve the crisis of faith which the exile had precipitated. He does this by a revitalized understanding of the tradition interpreted dynamically in the light of contemporary experience, and the center of the tradition remains always the revelation of divine power and grace in the exodus. The concrete historical situation of Israel in Babylon and the place of the exodus-theme in the tradition at that time would have made comparison with the original situation in Egypt inevitable, and it is therefore no surprise to find exodus-motifs recurring in these chapters. But the exilic situation was not a simple recurrence of that other 700 years previously in Egypt. Not only is there a great increase in the depth of the spatial and temporal perspective in which it is viewed, but there is an overpowering crisis of faith.

The visible center of world events around 540 B.C. was Cyrus, referred to more than once in the Deutero-Isaian oracles (see 41, 1-5; 41, 25-29; 45, 1-6; 48, 12-16). With Cyrus there emerged for Israel the problem of an inconceivably larger world which was in the process of finding a new unity, an *oecumene* in which she played no significant role at all. This involved basic tenets of the traditional faith: the covenant-fidelity of Yahweh, the possibility of a meaningful liturgy ("How shall we sing the Lord's song in a foreign land?": Ps. 137, 4), the reality of the universal power so often claimed for him by the pre-exilic prophets. The question of power was fundamental since it must have seemed to many Israelites that Yahweh had suffered humiliating defeat at the hands of the Babylonian city-god, Marduk, whose emblems and statues they had the mortification to see carried in procession through the streets (see Is. 45, 20; 46, 1-2). The so-called Cyrus Cylinder ascribes the call and victorious progress of the Persian king to Marduk,[6] and the polemic against this ascription which

[6] The text can be read in J. Pritchard, *Ancient Near Eastern Texts* (Princeton, [2]1955), pp. 315-16. For the background of the period as a whole, cf. C. F. Whitley, *The Exilic Age* (London, 1957); M. Noth, *The History of Israel* (London, [2]1960), pp. 289-316.

we hear more than once in these chapters shows us the prophet involving Israel in an incipient theology of history and power in history. The popular idea that Israel had been allotted to Yahweh as other nations had been to their respective gods, expressed in terms of Canaanite mythology in the Song of Moses (Deut. 32, 9) with which the exilic prophet was familiar, was still very much alive. It must have prompted the question: how can a national god survive in this greatly expanded world in which Israel was so far removed from the sources of power? How could their relationship with such a god, by which up till then they had lived, be maintained?

III

REACTUALIZATION OF THE EXODUS TRADITION

It would be misleading to present the prophet's answer to these problems in an oversystematic way by reducing the various and sometimes intricate patterns of thought to a common denominator and neglecting the possibility that there may be a development within the school of Second Isaiah in the use of traditional material. At the same time, the exodus theme is clearly pervasive. Without attempting an exhaustive identification of motifs from the tradition we might mention the following: the going out (43, 14-21; 48, 20-22; 52, 10; 55, 12), the mighty hand and arm of Yahweh (40, 10; 41, 10; 50, 2; 51, 9; 52, 10; 53, 1), the miraculous crossing of the sea and the river (43, 2; 44, 27; 51, 9-10), the way through the desert accompanied by the theophanous presence of Yahweh (40, 3-5), miracles of mercy in the desert (41, 17-20), entry into the promised land (49, 8-13).[7] An examination into how these motifs are used to interpret the theological dimension of contemporary events shows that the exodus has in the meantime become archetypal. It is seen as the

---

[7] For a more complete treatment with extensive bibliography, cf. J. Fischer, "Das Problem des neuen Exodus in Isaias c. 40-55," in *Theol. Quartalschrift* 110 (1929), pp. 111-30; B. W. Anderson, "Exodus Typology in Second Isaiah," in *Israel's Prophetic Heritage,* eds. B. W. Anderson and W. Harrelson (London, 1962), pp. 177-95.

primordial divine act containing within itself the revelation of the divine *dynamis*. We can trace the following stages in this process:

1. Exodus is the event prior to the covenant, the act of grace which made this unique relationship possible. The faith-relationship of the community still rested on the covenant; Yahweh still declares to Israel: "I am your God!" (41, 10; 48, 17; cf. the covenant-formula in Hosea 2, 25 and Jeremiah 31, 33) and affirms his covenant-love as of old (43, 4). Because of the exodus, the prophet can assure his brethren that Yahweh will keep covenant-faith and leave the future open. Thus eschatology in Second Isaiah is not an illegitimate extrapolation from a hopeless situation in the present, the outcome of historical despair, but is shown to be implicit in the primordial event upon which Israel's faith rested in the first place. Israel is therefore poised between past and future. Though the meaning of "the former things" is disputed,[8] in 43, 18 this expression refers to the exodus-event (cf. "the things of old" in parallelism, v. 19), the miraculous passage through the Sea of Reeds to which will correspond the return to the land. In this polarity of old and new exodus (cf. old and new covenant in Jeremiah 31, 31-34, possibly also from the exilic period) we seem to have in embryo the doctrine of the two ages and the justification for the New Testament presentation of the death of Jesus as exodus and inauguration of a new and final age.

2. In keeping with this, some of these exodus motifs are eschatologized. Thus the miracle of water in the desert is developed into the miraculous fertility of the *Endzeit* corresponding to the fertile garden of the *Urzeit*. Yahweh will "make her desert like Eden" (51, 3) and give his people "rivers in the desert" (43, 19f.; cf. 41, 17-20). As elsewhere in the Old Testament, this water imagery is symbolic of the outpoured Spirit (44, 3, with which cf. the quotation from Joel at Pentecost, Acts 2, 17ff. and the invitation to drink at the Feast of Booths, Jn. 7, 37-39) bringing

---

[8] In 41, 22; 42, 9 and 43, 9, the reference seems to be to the early career of Cyrus and his victorious progress down to 539. For this chronological polarity in Deutero-Isaiah in general, cf. A. Bentzen, "On the Ideas of 'the Old' and 'the New' in Deutero-Isaiah," in *Studia Theologica* I, 1-2 (1948), pp. 183-87.

"an everlasting salvation" (45, 17; 51, 6-8). Another example of this development is the way through the desert which becomes the processional way of the royal *parousia* (40, 3-5), in keeping with the royal ideology reflected here and there throughout these chapters. In both of these cases we can find the seeds of this development in the pre-exilic period.[9]

3. The principal means by which the exodus is given paradigmatic and archetypal value is its association with creation. Faith in God as creator is not however concerned here exclusively with a once-for-all act, but rather in the first place with the ability to act creatively *here and now*. Yahweh reveals himself as creative within the historical process and in the first place with regard to his people (43, 1. 7. 15; 44, 2; 51, 13. 16). Faith in Yahweh as creator of a people is anterior to faith in him as creator of the world, and Second Isaiah follows the Yahwist and possibly also the Priestly schools in placing the creation of Israel within the creation of the world. The technical term for this creative activity, the verb *bara'*, is used of the creation of Jacob = Israel (through the exodus) in the same way as in Genesis 1, 1. Perhaps the similarity of some hymnic passages praising the creator with the doxologies of Amos (4, 13; 5, 8-9; 9, 5-6) may be explained by a common derivation from the synagogue service of the exilic period.

The most interesting case of this association of exodus as creative act and the creation of the world occurs in what appears to be a stanza of a hymn (51, 9-11). Here the exodus theme is universalized by means of mythical categories; the mighty act in history is linked with the cosmogonic victory over the forces of chaos—power in history is associated with power over na-

---

[9] The paradisaic abundance of the messianic age in Amos 9, 13-15 may be a later addition, but there are suggestions of the same thing elsewhere (e.g., Hos. 2, 17. 23-25) corresponding to a genuinely ancient pattern of thinking. The motif of the processional way of the *parousia* occurs in Judges 5 and Psalm 68. For motifs connected with the royal messianism, cf. H. Gressmann, *Der Messias* (Göttingen, 1929), pp. 181ff.; S. Mowinckel, *He That Cometh* (Oxford, 1959). For a discussion on the latter's views on eschatology, cf. H. H. Rowley (ed.), *The Old Testament and Modern Study* (Oxford, 1956), pp. 189ff., 303ff.

ture.[10] There may have been some precedent for this in the earlier stages of the tradition—we find the smallest hint in the Song of Moses and Miriam (Ex. 15, 11)—especially if, as has been suggested, the creation recital of Genesis 1 displaced an earlier account which described creation as the outcome of a victory in the mythical *Urzeit*.[11] Here, at any rate, it was possible precisely because mythical thinking was beginning to lose its fascination for the Hebrew mind. The primeval monsters Rahab and Tannin, familiar figures in Semitic mythology, are elsewhere in the Old Testament cryptogrammatic for Egypt, the oppressive power *par excellence*.[12] The defeat of Chaos in the mythical cosmogony is superimposed on Yahweh's victory at the Sea of Reeds and the river Jordan, a superimposition all the more striking because the prophet's audience in that Sea (yam) and River (nahar) oppose the kingship of Ba'al in Canaanite mythology with which the Hebrews were familiar, just as Tiamat, monster of Chaos, opposes the kingship of Enlil (Marduk) in the Babylonian creation epic which some of the exiles must also have known.[13] By means of this mythical language the exodus is given the status of a primordial event in which the inherent *dynamis* is, in accordance with the functionality of mythical thinking, transferred to the present moment. This also implies an eschatological outlook, and in fact *bara'* is used of the future fulfillment —the flowering desert (41, 20), the "new things" (48, 7).

4. The whole problem of power and its source necessarily involves kingship since kingship was the basic repository of power. Already in the earlier stages of the tradition Yahweh deploys power in the exodus as a king (Ex. 15, 18; cf. Ps. 68,

[10] N. Lohfink, *Das Siegeslied am Schilfmeer* (Frankfurt, 1965), pp. 102ff., has some interesting reflections on this aspect of the exodus theme.

[11] P. Humbert, "La Rélation de Gen. I et du Ps. CIV avec la liturgie de nouvel an israelite," in *Rev. Hist. et Phil. rel.* 15 (1935), pp. 1-27.

[12] In Psalm 87, 4 Rahab is Egypt; in Ezekiel 29, 3 Tannin is Pharaoh. Cf. also Ezekiel 32, 2 and Psalm 74, 12-17.

[13] The creation epic was recited on the fourth day of the *akitu* festival; cf. *Dict. Bible Suppl.* VI, pp. 556-97; J. Pritchard, *op. cit.*, pp. 331-34. For royal ideology and the New Year Festival with relation to Isaiah 40-55, cf. J. Blenkinsopp, "The Unknown Prophet of the Exile," in *Scripture* 14 (1962), pp. 81-90, 109-18.

24. 34), and the kingship of Yahweh is prominent throughout the whole History of the Isaian school. Here, too, he is king and therefore the decider of destinies (41, 21; 44, 6). We have seen that Cyrus attributed his accession to Marduk who had been angry with Nabonidus for neglecting the *akitu* festival in which the king played the leading role and during which the creation epic *enuma elish* was recited.[14] Second Isaiah contains many echoes of the *akitu* cult-drama: procession, royal *parousia,* solemn proclamation of kingship ("your God reigns!": 52, 7), which may be interpreted as an appropriation by Yahweh of the royal ideology of the festival. Here we are at the center of the crisis of faith referred to above, since this deals with the reality of God's universal rule; and the exodus leading to the return has the purpose of leading men to acknowledge that rule and of actually bringing it about through a reconstituted Israel. The good news the herald proclaims in 52, 7 is the reign of God, and it is therefore no coincidence that the gospel, which *is* the advent of that reign, should open with a quotation from these chapters (Mk. 1, 3 and parallels).

By bringing out the paradigmatic character of the exodus and relating it both to God's creative activity in founding this world-order and his kingly rule in governing it, the prophet was able to build up a theological structure within which to present the divine activity both historical and metahistorical or eschatological. This was to be of fundamental importance for the presentation of the mission of Jesus and the new Israel to establish God's rule.

IV

NEW POSSIBILITIES FOR THE FUTURE

This new actualization of the old, canonical tradition brought with it a great deepening in the understanding of the divine activity in history, preparing for the New Testament interpretation of the final and central act of God in Jesus. It is already a

[14] In addition to the above, cf. E. Jenni, "Die Rolle des Kyros bei Deuterojesaja," in *Theol. Zeitschrift* 10 (1954), pp. 241-56.

first stage of interpretation by typology. The first Christian sermon will refer to the ministry of Jesus in exodus-language—
"the mighty works and wonders and signs which God did through
him" (Acts 2, 22), Luke will refer to the death of Jesus as an
exodus (9, 31), and other New Testament writers, especially
John, will continue this line of typological interpretation.[15] It
also brought with it a more profound insight into the nature of
the covenant-God. In Second Isaiah divine self-predication is
dominant: he reveals himself as the exodus-God, recapitulated
in the form "I am He!" which is best explained with reference
to the mysterious name revealed from the burning bush on the
eve of the exodus.[16] The exodus-God is, in the first place,
God-for-Israel, redeemer and savior. But since Israel's mission,
which could only be given to her in the suffering and estrange-
ment of exile, is essentially for the world, he is also universal
redeemer and savior. There are indications of a design to em-
brace all mankind in a universal salvation before the exilic period,
conspicuously in the Yahwist corpus, and ample warning for
Israel of the dangers of finding a false security in the covenant
relationship;[17] but here the promise of a universal saving plan
comes through clearly and insistently (see especially 42, 10; 45,
6. 14. 18-24). The tragedy of Israel was that, as the post-exilic
Book of Jonah shows, this message was so soon forgotten.

[15] It would take us beyond our scope to discuss the influence of Deutero-
Isaiah on exodus-typology in the New Testament. Consult J. Daniélou,
From Shadows to Reality (London, 1960), pp. 153-74; J. Guillet, "La
Thème de la Marche au desert dans l'Ancien et le Nouveau Testament,"
in *Recherches de Sciences Rel.* (1949), pp. 164ff.; P. Grelot, *Sens
chrétien de l'Ancien Testament* (Tournai, 1962), pp. 314, 492f.; H.
Sahlin in *The Root and the Vine*, ed. A. Fridrichsen (1953), pp. 18-95
(the exodus in Paul).

[16] Ex. 3, 14; Is. 41, 4; 43, 10. 13. 25; 46, 4; 48, 12; 51, 12. In view of
the numerous elements in the fourth gospel taken from Deutero-Isaiah,
the *ego eimi* of John 8, 24. 27 may be a revelation formula taken from its
use here. Consult E. Stauffer, *Jesus, Gestalt und Geschichte* (Bern, 1957),
pp. 30-46; C. H. Dodd, *The Interpretation of the Fourth Gospel* (Cambridge, 1955), pp. 349-50.

[17] A particularly interesting case of the latter is the statement in Amos
9, 7 that the Israelite exodus was not unique and that Yahweh had also
"brought up" other peoples.

Raymond Tournay, O.P. / *Jerusalem, Jordan*

Proverbs 1—9: A First Theological Synthesis of the Tradition of the Sages

he introduction to the book of Proverbs (1—9) forms a homogeneous section, except for 6, 1-19, which interrupts the sage's discourse, and 9, 7-12, which contains maxims added in the form of a commentary on v. 6. This first part of Proverbs may be dated from the beginning of the 5th century B.C.,[1] for it presupposes the same historical background as Third Isaiah (56ff.), which is roughly contemporary with the oracles of Haggai and Zechariah (518-515).

In five articles published thirty years ago,[2] A. Robert showed that Proverbs 1—9 reveals many points of contact with Deuteronomy and with the books of Jeremiah and Isaiah, particularly the latter. He points out that Isaiah 56ff.,[3] like Proverbs 1—9, attacks the abuses of a corrupt social order (Prov. 1, 16 corresponds to Is. 59, 7) and encourages the faithful in their sufferings at the hands of the impious. He connects Proverbs 1, 3 with

[1] Cf. P. Grelot, "La formation de l'Ancien Testament," in *Introduction à la Bible*, I, eds. A. Robert and A. Feuillet (Paris, ²1959), p. 825; B. Gemser, *Sprüche Salomos* (Tübingen, ²1963), p. 6.

[2] A. Robert, "Les attaches littéraires bibliques de Prov. I-IX," in *Rev. bibl.* 43 (1934), pp. 42-68, 172-204, 374-84; 44 (1935), pp. 344-65, 512-25; *idem*, "Littéraires (Genres)," in *Suppl. Dict. Bible* V (1957), pp. 413-16. Cf. R. Murphy, "The Wisdom Literature of the Old Testament," in *Concilium* 10: *The Human Reality of Sacred Scripture* (Glen Rock, N.J.: Paulist Press, 1965), pp. 126-40.

[3] A. Robert, *ibid.*, 44 (1935), pp. 358-65.

Isaiah 59, 14; Proverbs 1, 24-25 and 28-31 with Isaiah 65, 1-2. 12-15 and 66, 3-4, verses which describe the punishments of the wicked. He quotes Isaiah 57, 6 in connection with the description of the adulteress in Proverbs 7, 10ff., and he sees some analogy between the mysterious envoy of Isaiah 61, 1 and the Wisdom-prophet of Proverbs 1, 20ff. and 9, 1ff. who proclaims judgment and salvation. Finally, the banquet of the Lady Wisdom (9, 1ff.) is reminiscent of Isaiah 65, 11ff., both passages echoing Isaiah 55, 1-3, which concludes Second Isaiah (composed, as we know, shortly before the end of the Babylonian exile).

If Proverbs 1—9 dates from the first decades after the return of the Jewish exiles to Sion, it is rather earlier than Malachi (dated in the middle of the 5th century). Malachi 2, 10ff. and Proverbs 2, 16-17 both invoke the covenant with regard to marriage with a foreign woman. Proverbs 3, 9, the only passage in Proverbs 1—9 to mention an act of religious worship, corresponds to Malachi 3, 10, which stresses the payment of the tithe and a pledge of the divine blessings. The suffering endured by the just is a trial inflicted by God on those whom he loves, and whom he treats as a father does his children (Mal. 3, 17; Prov. 3, 11-12).[4] The book of Job, however, cannot be earlier than Proverbs 1—9, for it raises acutely the problem of the sufferings of the just man, while Job's friends, apart from Elihu, defend the classical position of the sages, which is that of Proverbs 1—9, on earthly retribution. Moreover, Job 28, 15ff. seems to depend on Proverbs 8, 10-11, and Job 28, 23-27 on Proverbs 8, 22ff., while Job 15, 7 and 25, 10 repeat Proverbs 8, 25 and 27.

It was, then, at the beginning of the 5th century that a scribe of Jerusalem, having resolved to edit all the ancient proverbs, composed an appropriate introduction on the blessings and charms of the Lady Wisdom. He concluded this compilation with an epilogue (31, 10ff.), an alphabetic poem in praise of the ideal wife, the resourceful woman, the feminine embodiment of

[4] *Ibid.*, 44 (1935), pp. 506-08. The expression "table of Yahweh" (Mal. 1, 7) recalls Wisdom's "table" (Prov. 9, 2).

the sage; this portrait reflects 9, 1-6 and contains about ten characteristic words used in Proverbs 1—9. Now, at the same time, scribes and priests were editing the prophetical corpus by completing the "former prophets" (cf. Zech. 1, 4; 7, 12); they were then composing the endings of Amos, Micah and Zephaniah, as well as Micah 4—5, Ezekiel 38—39, 22, the additions to the books of Isaiah (11, 10-16; 12; 34—35, etc.) and Jeremiah (3, 14-18; 10, 1-16, etc.). The author of the "little apocalypse" of Isaiah (34, 35) also refers to the "book of the Lord" (34, 14), which is no doubt Isaiah 31, 21-22, announcing the imminent fall of Babylon. The end of the 5th century saw the completion of the juridical corpus, the Torah, which was promulgated by Ezra in 398 and included what is called the "priestly" history (Gen. 1, etc.). The psalmody was then enriched by many psalms composed for the liturgy of the Second Temple. It was in this age of intense literary activity (which was also the age of Pericles, Buddha and Confucius) that the synthesis of the tradition of the sages was constructed in Proverbs 1—9. A work of imitation but also of originality, this little book testifies to the astonishing vitality of Yahwism, which was able to assimilate the teaching of the learned, which for a long time had been handed down orally in the homes of the wealthy and at the royal court.

I

IMITATION AND ANTHOLOGICAL STYLE

Proverbs 1—9 and the Ancient Proverbs

The author of Proverbs 1—9 made considerable use of the maxims of his forerunners whom he was editing. His prologue (1, 1-6) reminds us of the "words of the wise" (22, 17-21); these certainly date from the end of the Judean monarchy, and in their opening (22, 17—23, 11) they have many affinities with the Sentences of Amenemopeh.[5] This ancient collection (22,

---

[5] Cf. B. Couroyer, "L'origine égyptienne de la Sagesse d'Amenemopé," in *Rev. bibl.* 70 (1963), pp. 208-24.

17ff.) is placed between two great "Salomonian" collections (10—22, 16 and 25—29). The group 14, 26—16, 15 and the collection 22, 17ff. have some affinities with Deuteronomy. The group 14, 26ff., moreover, presumes that a king is still in existence, as does 24, 21, where the king is mentioned after Yahweh; this king might well be Josiah, the holiest king of Israel (2 Kg. 23, 25).[6] The second great collection, 25—29, is no more homogeneous; "the men of Hezekiah, king of Judah" (25, 1) are supposed to have transcribed part of it, originating in the northern kingdom, and to have introduced it to Judah after the fall of Samaria.[7] The section 28—29, which is more religious than 25—27, contains proverbs in antithetical parallels, whereas in 25—27 the parallels are mostly synonymous (as in 1—9 and 14, 26—22, 16). The king is mentioned in very general terms, and the Torah seems to have been already written down.[8] If the group 28—29 (perhaps, also, even 27, 11-27) is post-exilic,[9] we may wonder whether it has not the same origin as 1—9. If 8, 14 seems to be inspired by the messianic oracle of Isaiah 11, 2-5, similarly 29, 4 and 14 speak of the king as if he were the Messiah. Further, the letter *taw*, the last letter of the alphabet, appears four times in the last verse of chapter 29; Job 31, 40 uses the same device to indicate the "end" of the words of Job.

Among the many points borrowed by Proverbs 1—9 from the older collections we find the following: the crown or "garland" of the wise (1, 9; 9, 9; 14, 18. 24); the tree of life (3, 18; 11, 30; 13, 12; 15, 4); the expressions "inhabit the land" (2, 21; 10, 30) and "happy";[10] wisdom more precious than gold or silver (3, 14; 8, 19; 16, 16) or than coral (RSV: jewels) (8, 11; 20,

---

[6] Cf. R. Tournay, "Recherches sur la chronologie des Psaumes," in *Rev. bibl.* 66 (1959), pp. 188-90.

[7] Cf. H. Cazelles, "Les débuts de la Sagesse en Israël," in *Les Sagesses du Proche-Orient ancien* (Paris, 1963), p. 31.

[8] Cf. 28, 4. 7. 9; 29, 18. In 13, 14 "Torah" denotes the teaching of the sage, as in Prov. 1-9 (1, 3; 3, 1; 4, 2; 6, 20; 7, 2). Cf. A. Robert, "Le yahwisme de Prov. X, 1—XXII, 16; XXV-XXIX," in *Mémorial Lagrange* (Paris, 1940), pp. 170-73.

[9] It has many doublets (cf. 14, 26—16, 15) and it uses a direct and apostrophic style (cf. 1-9; 22, 17—24, 22).

[10] Prov. 3, 13; 8, 32. 34; cf. 14, 21; 16, 20; 20, 7; 28, 14; 29, 18; Pss. 1, 1; 111, 1; 119, 1; 128, 1.

15; 31, 10); the allusion to the "neighbor";[11] not envying the wicked;[12] following the sure path (3, 23; 10, 9); God loves the humble (3, 34; 15, 33); the reckless and imprudent go down to the abode of the "shades" (9, 18; 21, 16). Young men must, above all, avoid the "foreign woman", the wife of another man (2, 16-22; 5, 1-23; 6, 23—7, 27); these long exhortations are developments of 22, 14 and 23, 27 (cf. 29, 3). The portrait of the perfect wife (31, 10ff.) resumes the theme of 11, 6; 18, 22 and 19, 14. Verse 24, 13 had already spoken of the wisdom with which a house is built; 14, 1 went further, contrasting Wisdom and Folly, the one building, the other pulling down, her own house. The author of Proverbs 1—9 concludes his discourse by presenting Wisdom as a hostess, inviting all simple souls to her table, whereas Lady Folly sits outside and lures the passers-by to their death, like the foreign woman of 7, 5ff. Our author, while making use of the ancient maxims, here transposes the conclusion of the Second Isaiah (55, 1-3) and faces his disciple with an alternative: it would be hard to find a better way of disposing men's hearts to accept the teaching of the chapters which follow.[13]

Proverbs 1—9 and Deuteronomy

As is proved by many didactic elements found in Deuteronomy, it was near the end of the monarchy that Wisdom and the Torah began to be interfused.[14] The verb *lamad* (whence the word *Talmud*), "to teach, to learn", appears seventeen times in Deuteronomy, although it is not found in the rest of the Penta-

[11] Cf. 3, 28-29; 6, 1. 3. 29; 25, 9; 27, 17. In regard to the end of the monarchy, Leviticus 19, 18 (the law of holiness) bids men to love their neighbor as themselves.

[12] Cf. 3, 31; 23, 17; 24, 1. 19; Pss. 37, 1-4; 73, 3.

[13] Cf. A. Robert, *art. cit., Rev. bibl.* 43 (1934), p. 384. The banquet of Wisdom is simply a variant of the messianic banquet. Cf. A. Feuillet, "Les thèmes bibliques majeurs du discours sur le pain de vie (Jn. 6)," in *Nouv. Rev. Théol.* 82 (1960), pp. 918-20.

[14] Cf. J. Malfroy, "Sagesse et Loi dans le Deutéronome," in *Vetus Testamentum* 15 (1965), pp. 49-65. M. Weinfeld thinks that Deuteronomy represents the fusion of the Torah and Wisdom, brought about by the schools of humanist scribes (cf. *Zeitschr. f. alttest. Wiss.* 73 [1961], pp. 244, 333; 74 [1962], pp. 86, 97; 78 [1966], p. 130).

teuch. N. Lohfink[15] points out the characteristic use of this word in Deuteronomy 4, 1-14. The "discourses" of Moses are addressed to the heart (conscience) in fatherly exhortation; they are direct in style, bidding men to obey God and trust in him with filial fear. Following Hosea and in the manner of Jeremiah, Deuteronomy reminds us that true religion is based on the knowledge of God, who speaks to Israel as a father to his son, in order to educate him (8, 5; cf. 1, 31). Now the expression "my son",[16] which occurs ten times in Proverbs 10—27, appears no less than fifteen times in Proverbs 1—9, which is one long paternal discourse. Further, Deuteronomy embodies a series of prohibitions or "abominations" (seventeen cases, twelve of which are "abominations to Yahweh"), legal stipulations with a certain didactic character.[17] Proverbs has this expression twenty-one times. Proverbs 3, 32 declares: "The perverse man is an abomination to Yahweh" (cf. 6, 16; 8, 7). The chief inspiration of Proverbs 1—9 seems to have been Deuteronomy 6, 4-9,[18] and to such an extent that C. W. Buchanan[19] considers this section of Proverbs to be the oldest example of midrashic interpretation of that heart of Israel's legal code, the "Shema Israel". The earliest rabbinical commentaries had already associated these two groups of texts. Modern exegetes emphasize the deuteronomic tone of Proverbs 2, 20-22; 3, 1-3. 23; 7, 2-3. This would give us a first attempt at *halakhah*, rules of conduct showing men how to "walk" (*halakh*) in the way laid down by God.

Proverbs 1—9 and Jeremiah

Wisdom personified speaks to men in a prophetic style evoking the "day" of judgment: 1, 20-33 recalls Jeremiah 30, 7; 50, 27. 31, etc. Jeremiah speaks of the tablet of the heart (17, 1;

---

[15] *Höre, Israël!* (Die Welt der Bibel) (Düsseldorf, 1965), pp. 98-101.

[16] Only once in Qohelet (12, 12); 22 times in Sirach.

[17] Cf. J. L'Hour, "Les interdits to'eba dans le Deutéronome," in *Rev. bibl.* 71 (1964), pp. 482-84.

[18] The parallel 11, 18-22 is presumed to be a conclusion composed later.

[19] "Midrashim pré-tannaïtes. A propos de Prov. I-IX," in *Rev. bibl.* 72 (1965), pp. 227-39. The midrash is an ancient literary form (cf. Exod. 16); on the midrash and the *halakhah*, cf. A. Robert and A. Feuillet, *Introduction à la Bible*, I (Paris, ²1959), pp. 174, 722.

31, 33), a figure adopted in Proverbs 3, 3; 7, 3. Proverbs 3, 31-34 contrasts the violent with the humble, of whom Jeremiah was the perfect type. "Often warned (Jer. 26, 4), [Israel] has always refused to listen to Yahweh's words (Jer. 5, 3; 7, 25-26; 25, 4ff.; 29, 19; Is. 65, 12). Ruin will befall him (Jer. 25, 9ff.) and in that day Yahweh will be deaf to his cries and will laugh him to scorn (Jer. 11, 1; Hos. 5, 6; Mic. 3, 4). Like the prophets, Wisdom also speaks in the crowded places (Jer. 11, 6; 7, 2; 17, 19ff.; 22, 2-6; 26, 2)."[20] Proverbs 1—9 is inspired not only by Jeremiah, whose book was of course edited by the deuteronomic school, but also by the prophetic oracles. Thus the editor of Proverbs enables his independent teaching, with its distinctive values, to benefit from the riches contained in the Law and the prophets.[21]

II

A THEOLOGICAL WISDOM

Wisdom as Justice and the Fear of God

Not content with utilizing and imitating the older scriptures, the author of Proverbs 1—9 raises his thinking to the level of the strictly theological. Wisdom, like riches, was originally seen as a gift of God (cf. Prov. 2, 6). But Solomon practiced idolatry (cf. Deut. 17, 16ff.); Egypt had its sages (Is. 19, 12); the king of Tyre, wise as he was (Ezek. 28, 3), was overthrown by God. Isaiah was the first to apply to God the epithet of "wise" (31, 2), but this was in connection with the punishment of the wicked. According to him, God ascribes wisdom to the davidic Messiah (11, 2), but together with the fear of God. At this period, in fact, the sage is still only a learned man, an official at the court, a counselor of the king and his princes, not a member of the levitical priesthood. Wisdom is therefore associated with

[20] A. Barucq, *Le livre des Proverbes* (Paris, 1964), p. 53. In this work Proverbs 1, 23 and Isaiah 44, 3 are compared.

[21] From the Persian era onward, the "anthological" style is increasingly characteristic of the biblical writings, especially the lyrics and psalmody. Cf. A. Robert and R. Tournay, *Le Cantique des Cantiques* (Paris, 1963), pp. 10ff. (Song 4, 11. 12. 15 may be compared with Prov. 5, 3. 15. 16; Song 5, 6 with Prov. 1, 28; Song 6, 9 with Prov. 4, 3 and 31, 28; Song 8, 7 with Prov. 6, 31).

law. The words "just" or "justice" occur sixty-five times in the first great "Salomonian" collection and nine times in the second; these are contemporary with Amos, Isaiah and Micah.

But in Ezekiel, that humanist priest, we have a new type of thinker; his disciple, the Second Isaiah, opens the way to universalist and cosmic perspectives. The author of Proverbs 1— 9, in his turn, finally exorcises wisdom by defining its principle as the fear of God, the fundamental virtue of the "poor of Yahweh". Shortly before the time of the exile, Proverbs 15, 33 had said that the fear of God is the school of wisdom. According to 13, 14 and 14, 27 (cf. 19, 23), wisdom and the fear of God are equally the fountain of life. These proverbs paved the way for the famous formula that concludes the preamble to the proverbs (1, 1-7): "The fear of the Lord is the beginning of wisdom." Repeated in 9, 10 (a probable addition; cf. also 2, 5-6), Job 28, 28 and Psalm 111, 10 (in the form of a conclusion), and also in Sirach 1, 14. 20, this statement emphasizes the profoundly religious aspect of Israelite wisdom from this period onward.

Wisdom as the Daughter of God

In Proverbs 8, Wisdom recites her own praise. First she speaks of her relations with men, especially with kings (15—16; cf. 20, 26) and ascribes to herself the qualities of the davidic anointed one (Is. 11, 2; Jer. 23, 5).[22] Those who seek her will find her; she loves those who love her. These two expressions recall Deuteronomy and some of the oracles.[23] The second part of this "prosopopeia" treats of Wisdom's relations with God. We have already learned from 3, 19-30 that Yahweh had founded the

---

[22] Cf. H. Cazelles, "L'enfantement de la Sagesse en Prov. VIII," in *Sacra Pagina*, I (Gembloux, 1959), pp. 510-15. In Prov. 8, 14 the term "wisdom" of Is. 11, 2 is replaced by a word meaning realistic good sense, but "wisdom" appears in Job 12, 13 which applies these qualities to God.

[23] Deut. 4, 29. 37; 7, 8. 13; Hos. 11, 1; Jer. 29, 13; 31, 3; Is. 54, 8; 55, 6. The second expression is found on some Egyptian scarabs (cf. E. Drioton, "La religion égyptienne," in *Histoire des Religions* (Paris, 1955), p. 94. At all periods the sages of Israel were influenced by Egypt far more than they were by Phoenicia (on this latter point, cf. M. Dahood, *Proverbs and Northwest Semitic Philology* [Rome, 1963], pp. 3-18).

earth by wisdom and established the heavens by understanding.[24] Here this royal Wisdom displays her titles of nobility. She is not a creature, but exists before creation; formed and brought forth by God, she is his own possession, acquired by way of generation (cf. Gen. 4, 1; Deut. 32, 6), as some versions have understood it.[25] She is therefore present at the creation without actively participating in it; like a little girl (*Aquila* translates "nursling"), an "Infanta" (this is A. Gelin's word), she plays and gambols gracefully, like David before the ark, in the presence of her father and on the face of the earth (cf. Bar. 3, 37). In the beginning of time Lady Wisdom was really only a young princess, but already so attractive! Perhaps the author of this allegory remembered Ezekiel 16, describing the origin of Israel, spouse of Yahweh, or he may have thought of Maât, the personification of justice, whom the Egyptians held to be the daughter of the sungod.[26]

However that may be, this wonderful poem to some extent recalls Second Isaiah (40, 9. 12; 45, 19. 22; cf. Deut. 32, 18), and it prepares for Genesis 1 (cf. Pss. 90, 2; 104) which takes the same optimistic view of the organization of the world. Thus the old cosmogonies are stripped of their myths. Moreover, the messianic hope is shown to be reposed on God alone, at a time when the monarchy had disappeared. Wisdom, like the Messiah, the Son of God, plays the part of mediator: she is sent to men to bring them happiness. As the confidant of the creator, she knows the secrets of the universe; endowed with charm and nobility, she has the right to teach men and be heard by them. As God's

[24] A passage repeated in Jer. 10, 12 and 51, 15 (post-exilic additions).

[25] Aquila, Symmachus, Theodotion, Vulgate. However, the Septuagint, Targum and Syriac imply a created being. We do not know the Hebrew verb translated by "he has created me" in the Greek of Sirach 24, 9. The translation of the word *amôn* (8, 30) by "architect, master workman (demiurge?)" scarcely fits the context which speaks of play and delights. Cf. A. Gelin, "Le chant de l'Infante," in *Bible et vie chretienne* 7 (1954), pp. 89-95; A. Hulsbosch, *Sagesse créatrice et éducatrice* (Bibliotheca Augustiniana) (Rome, 1963), pp. 40-44 (he compares Is. 60, 4; 66, 12; Jer. 31, 20; Zech. 8, 5); R. B. Y. Scott, *Proverbs, Ecclesiastes* (The Anchor Bible, 1965), p. 72 (for *omen* understand "uniting [all]").

[26] H. Donner, "Die religionsgeschichtlichen Ursprünge von Prov. Sal. 8," in *Zeitschr. f. Ägyptische Sprache* 82 (1958), p. 17.

companion (Wis. 9, 4 makes her share the divine throne!), she is to become the companion of men, God's children, who will call her "my sister" (7, 4). Those who find her find life and God's favor, a theme already outlined in 10, 17; 13, 14 and 16, 22.

Virtualities and Limitations of This Doctrine

The prophets derived the Yahwist morality from a history of salvation; here the morality is derived from the very structure of creation, the wonderful work of a wise God. As early as the time of Josiah the ethic of the sages was expressly Yahwist and religious; now it develops into a theology, the knowledge of a God who is creator and providence. Here the ancient didactic tradition of Israel attains a summit, embracing even the messianic themes. It constitutes an "acquired knowledge", a "received" doctrine,[27] but one which is always progressing.

If Psalm 104, 24 is the only text of the psalms that ascribes wisdom to God in his role of creator, Job 28 insists on the mysterious transcendence of such wisdom. In the Hellenistic era, Baruch 3, 9—4, 4 and Sirach 24 identify Wisdom with the Law, the exclusive property of Israel, thus completing the process begun by Deuteronomy. Wisdom 7, 25ff. continues these speculations, emphasizing the divine character of Wisdom, beloved of God as a spouse, and assimilated to the Spirit of Yahweh. Through the medium of these texts, Proverbs 8 is the source of the Pauline and Johannine doctrine of the incarnate Word, the Wisdom of God (1 Cor. 1, 24), the firstborn of creation (Col 1, 15).[28]

Such a summit, however, also marks a limit on which believers

[27] Cf. 1, 5; 4, 2; 9, 9. The first use of the word is in Deuteronomy 32, 2 (the end of the exile; cf. Is. 40—55); it later appears in Job 11, 4 and Sirach 8, 8 (Is. 29, 24 is post-exilic).

[28] The doctrine of Wisdom, adumbrated in the Old Testament, prepared the way for the doctrine of the Trinity (cf. Bible de Jérusalem [Paris, 1956], pp. 810, footnote e, 877, footnote a); however, its influence on the theme of the Son of Man (Book of Daniel) is still the subject of discussion (cf. the article by J. Coppens in Suppl. to Vetus Testamentum 3 [1955], pp. 33-41).

would stumble, scandalized by the apparent good fortune of the wicked and the sufferings of the innocent (Mal. 3, 15; Ps. 37, 1). Deliberately optimistic, the author of Proverbs 1—9 holds fast to the system of earthly rewards. Soon after his time the Book of Job debated this tormenting problem at length, without providing a solution to belie the facts, and ended with a sublime act of faith and humility.[29] During the Persian era the heart-searchings of some psalmists, for whom the essence of happiness lay in life with God (Pss. 16, 10; 49, 16; 73, 24), tentatively led the way to a new stage of revelation, still unknown to Qohelet (8, 1-14) or to Ben Sirach some decades later: belief in the resurrection of the just (Dan. 12, 2; 2 Macc. 7, 9; 12, 43; 14, 46) and the immortality of the soul (Wis. 2, 33; 3, 9; 6, 19). But before this could come about, Israel had to undergo the first religious persecution of her history. How could God, in his perfect justice, fail to give life to those who died for his sake? From the days of the Maccabees the dilemma of life or death, light or darkness (Prov. 4, 18-19; 5, 23; 9, 6; cf. 10, 16; Jer. 21, 8; Deut. 30, 15) acquires a new and singularly dramatic meaning. More than three centuries after Proverbs 1—9, revelation took a decisive step forward, with belief in the rewards of the afterlife.[30]

As an apologia for traditional Yahwism—under the aspect, and with the peculiar resources, of a doctrine of wisdom—Proverbs 1—9 represents an important stage in the evolution of Israel's religious thought. The teacher of wisdom who made it the imposing prologue to the didactic corpus of the proverbs constantly exploits the ancient scriptures by transposing them into a new perspective, that of creation. The ancient wisdom of the chosen people thus culminates in an original synthesis in which the religious genius of post-exilic Judaism is asserted for the first time.

[29] Cf. R. Tournay, "Le procès de Job ou l'innocent devant Dieu," in *Vie Spir.* 95 (1956), pp. 339-54; *idem*, "El processo de Job," in *Selecciones de Teologia* 17 (1966), pp. 93-96.

[30] Cf. P. Grelot, "La révélation de bonheur dans l'Ancien Testament," in *Lumière et Vie* 52 (1961), pp. 19-35; *idem*, "L'eschatologie de la Sagesse et les Apocalypses juives," in *A la rencontre de Dieu* (Mémorial Gelin) (Le Puy, 1961), pp. 165-78.

Frans Neirynck/*Louvain, Belgium*

The Tradition of the Sayings of Jesus: Mark 9, 33-50

B ible readers have gradually become aware of the fact that the canonical gospels were preceded by a long prehistory and that the discourses of Jesus are mainly collections of sayings which circulated independently. There is often no logical inner connection between these sayings; they are merely an assemblage of statements that are identical or similar, and this would point to the fact that the association of these words happened during the early stages of the—still Aramaic—oral tradition. Here Mark 9, 33-50 may well serve as a paradigm, particularly since the article by L. Vaganay in 1953.[1] This study offers an excellent starting point for further investiga-

[1] L. Vaganay, "Le schématisme du discors communautaire à la lumière de la critique des sources," in *Revue biblique* 60 (1953), pp. 203-44; also in *Le problème synoptique* (Bibliothèque de théologie III/I) (Paris/ Tournai, 1954), pp. 361-425. Cf. R. Schnackenburg, "Mark 9, 33-50," in *Synoptische Studien. Festschrift A. Wikenhauser* (Munich, 1953), pp. 184-206, in which the author defends the priority of Mark and does not exclude editing by the evangelist (cf. 13, 33-37; 8, 34-37. 38; 4, 21-25); A. Descamps, "Du discours de Marc IX, 33-50 aux paroles de Jésus," in *La formation des évangiles. Problème synoptique et Formgeschichte* (Recherches Bibliques, 2) (Bruges/Louvain, 1957), pp. 152-77, which provides the history of the transmission of the sayings. For Matthew, cf. W. Pesch, "Die sogenannte Gemeindeordnung Mt. 18," in *Biblische Zeitschrift* 7 (1963), pp. 220-35; W. Trilling, *Das Wahre Israel. Studien zur Theologie des Matthäus-Evangeliums* (Munich, 1964), pp. 106-23. These and other studies deserve fuller treatment but I cannot do more here than introduce them.

tion, even though it may appear that the author went about it a little rashly. The *key-word* association does not allow us on every occasion to pass from the Greek text to the Aramaic transmission, and it is significant that even the editors of the gospels were not unaware of this. Moreover, many will not be able to follow Vaganay in his reconstruction of the basic document, for which he uses all three synoptic versions. Yet, it must be immediately added that Vaganay's hypothetical document departs only slightly from Mark's text.[2] Here I will take the text of Mark as the starting point of the discussion. This cannot, of course, be done independently of a definite view of the synoptic problem in general. Indeed, it appears to me that the new studies of Mark and Luke now allow a firmer reliance on the current opinion about the priority of Mark.

Mark 9, 33-50

33. And they came to Capernaum; and when he was in the house he asked them, *"What were you discussing on the way?"* 34. But they were silent; *for on the way they had discussed with one another who was the greatest.* 35. And he sat down and called the twelve; and he said to them, "If any one would be *first,* he must be last of all and servant of all. 36. And he took a child, and put him in the midst of them; and taking him in his arms, he said to them, 37. "Whoever receives *one such child in my name* receives me; and whoever receives me, receives not me but him who sent me."

38. John said to him, "Teacher, we saw a man casting out demons *in your name,* and we forbade him, because he was not following us." 39. But Jesus said, "Do not forbid him; for no one who does a mighty work *in my name* will be able soon after to speak evil of me. 40. For he that is not against

[2] Apart from the omissions of Luke 9, 48c (after v. 35a) and Matthew 18, 10. 14 (after v. 41), Mark is said to have made some slight alterations in v. 35c (cf. Mt. 23, 11), v. 36b (add.), v. 41a (cf. Mt. 10, 42) and v. 42 (cf. Mt. 18, 6).

us is for us. 41. For truly, I say to you, whoever gives you a cup of water to drink, because you bear *the name* of Christ, will by no means lose his reward.

42. "Whoever *causes one of these little ones* who believe in me *to sin,* it would be *better* for him if a great millstone were hung round his neck and he were *thrown* into the sea. 43. And if your hand *causes* you *to sin,* cut it off; it is *better* for you *to enter life* maimed than with two hands to go *to hell,* to the unquenchable *fire.* 45. And if your foot *causes* you *to sin,* cut it off; it is *better* for you *to enter life* lame than with two feet *to be thrown into hell.* 47. And if your eye *causes* you *to sin,* pluck it out; it is better for you *to enter* the kingdom of God with one eye than with two eyes *to be thrown into hell,* 48. where their worm does not die, and the *fire* is not quenched. 49. For every one will be *salted* with *fire.* 50. *Salt* is *good;* but if the *salt* has *lost its saltness,* how will you season it? Have *salt* in yourselves, *and be at peace with one another."*

It is perhaps useful to point out that, whatever the problems of the context of this passage, the evangelist took it as a literary unit. This is clear from v. 50 where the point of mutual peace links up with the starting point, the disciples' quarrel about precedence. It becomes even clearer when we put the text in the framework of the gospel. Mark 9, 33-50 is part of a broader context which deals with Jesus' journey from Galilee to Jerusalem. It begins with Peter's confession, preceded and prepared by the section about the loaves (6, 31—8, 26), while Jesus' appearance in Jerusalem in 11, 1ff. opens the next phase. The construction of this section (8, 27—10, 52) is obviously dominated by the three prophecies of the passion (8, 31-33; 9, 30-32; 10, 32-34), followed each time by an instruction for the disciples (8, 34—9, 1; 9, 33-50; 10, 35-45), with which particular pericopes are connected: the transfiguration and the healing of the young epileptic (9, 2-29), the passage about divorce, the blessing of the children and the conversation with the rich man (10, 1-31), and, finally, the cure of the blind Bartimeus (10, 46-52). This construction puts the statement about the precedence among the disciples on a line with the words about "taking up one's cross" and "losing one's soul" (8, 34-35), about the chalice, baptism and being a servant (10, 38-40. 43-44). The theme of imitating Christ's passion thus links the three passages. "If any one would" of 9, 35 links up with "if any one would" of 8, 34-35 and "whoever would" of 10, 43-44. We may assume that the evangelist was aware of this parallelism. In any case, it seems that Luke, the first exegete of Mark's gospel, brought 9, 33-35 and 10, 42-45 together; one can compare this with Luke 22, 24-27.

Seen in this light, v. 35 is certainly not the least important verse in this passage. It offers Jesus' reply to the question about precedence and at the same time introduces an instruction: "He sat down. . . ." (cf. 10, 1: after that instruction he stands up). Then follows the scene with the child that includes the saying: "Whoever receives one such child in my name. . . ." (v. 37). With this verse a double series of Jesus' sayings are connected. "In my name" links the "name" sayings of vv. 38-41 together. The last saying not only resumes the term "name" by way of summary conclusion but also the thought of v. 37. "One such child" in that same verse provides the connecting point for the saying about scandal of v. 42 ("one of these little ones"). The verses that follow are clearly interconnected: vv. 42 and 43-48 (to give scandal, *to cause sin*) and vv. 49-50 (*salt*) are linked with each other through vv. 48 and 49 (*fire*). The whole is rounded off with the theme of the end of v. 50 (cf. vv. 33-34).

While the sayings of vv. 35, 37 and 39 correspond to a narrative introduction, they become an uninterrupted discourse of Jesus from v. 39 to v. 50, which leaves the intervention of John in v. 38 far behind. This is curious because in Mark's gospel the apocalyptic narrative of chapter 13 is the only great discourse of Jesus. The parables of 4, 1-34 are interrupted by short narrative notices that point to an assemblage of loose elements.[3] The same can be seen in the text about ritual purity (7, 6-23).[4]

[3] Cf. 4, 1-2. 9a. 10-11a. 13a. 21a. 24a. 26a. 30a. 33-34.
[4] Cf. 7, 6a. 9a. 14a. 17-18a. 20a.

The missionary discourse of 6, 7-11 only passes in v. 9 to direct speech and also contains in v. 10a the phrase "and he said to them". Apart from shorter texts such as the reply to the question about fasting in 2, 19-22 and the texts already mentioned of 8, 34—9, 1 (particularly 9, 1a!) and 10, 42-45, there only remains the self-defense of 3, 23-29. But perhaps we have to take into account here the introductory formula of v. 28a[5] which, together with the evangelist's comments in v. 30, detaches somewhat the saying about blaspheming against the Holy Spirit from vv. 23-27. For the rest, it should be mentioned here that the agreements between the parallel texts of Matthew and Luke (11, 17-23!) are so striking that, with most exegetes, I suspect that they derive from Q (*Quelle,* which is the name given to the common source of Matthew and Luke). Even without going into the problem of the relations between Mark and Q, we may rightly speak here of an archaic tradition. Things are different for Mark 9, 33-50 inasmuch as there are only parallel texts from Q for 50a (Lk. 14, 34-35; cf. Mt. 5, 13).

Insofar as the parallel texts of Mark 9, 33-50 are concerned, Luke 9, 46-50 is limited to vv. 33-41, and even then vv. 33a, 35 (cf. Luke 9, 48c), 39b and 41 are lacking. The sayings about scandal and the words about the salt are missing from this context. After Luke has followed Mark's text from Peter's confession onward, he passes on to his own central section of the so-called journey narrative (9, 51—18, 14) and then takes up Mark's narrative again with the blessing of the children (Mk. 10, 13ff.). On his side, Matthew closely follows Mark's matter and sequence (Mk. 6, 14) from 14, 1 on (after the curious transpositions in the first part of his gospel). There are, it is true, a few omissions and some smaller additions, among which are particularly the texts about Peter (14, 28-31: the miracle on the lake; 16, 17-19: the promise given to Peter; 17, 24-27: the temple tax). This last pericope immediately precedes our text and gives in vv. 24 and 25 the parallel to the introductory notice which situates the

---

[5] "Truly, I say to you"; cf. 9, 1; 10, 15. 29; 11, 23; 14, 9, all of which are equally "additions".

event in the house in Capernaum (Mk. 9, 33a). Then follows Matthew 18, 1-9 which corresponds to Mark 9, 33b-37. 42-48 (the passage about the miracles "in his name" and the words about the salt are missing), but with differences which I must still discuss and which are included in the wider contents of the discourse of Matthew 18, 1-35.

Over against the shorter versions of Matthew and Luke, most authors uphold the priority of Mark 9, 33-50. Some moderate this view by assuming a common source or a (relative) mutual independence of the evangelists. Others do not hesitate to ascribe the priority to the canonical Matthew. Sometimes, too, there is a desire to detach the study of the sayings of Jesus from the supposedly hopeless problems of source criticism. Some attempt to detach the saying of Jesus from its context in the three gospels; they seek to understand it directly in the framework of Jesus' preaching and the nondescript environment of the early Christians. However, we should not forget that the last stage of the transmission of Jesus' sayings—namely, their use by the evangelists—will always remain for us the least hypothetical phase. And however attractive the direct method may appear to some, the only responsible approach to the historical sayings of Jesus must start with a comparative analysis of the various ways in which they were edited. If it then appears that Matthew 18, 1-9 and Luke 9, 46-50, with their more closely knitted context of the sayings, are secondary revisions of Mark, then it becomes a risky undertaking to place them in an earlier tradition, bypassing Mark. If the independent witness of Matthew and Luke collapses, it becomes difficult to prove that in Mark 9, 33-50 we have a collection of sayings prior to Mark. If we take Mark's priority seriously, then it becomes indeed a delicate task to sever tradition from the editing process. This holds as much for our text as for the grouping of the narrative matter.[6] Up to a point the "discourse" of Jesus in Mark 9 is a unique case. This means

---

[6] For example, the day at Capernaum (1, 21-39), the series of disputes (2, 1—3, 6), the cycle of miracles (4, 35—5, 43) and the passage about the loaves (6, 21—8, 26).

that we do not have the comparative matter which we need to detach the ordering by means of key words from the editing by the evangelist. Is the process in fact so very different from his way of linking parables together by means of "and he said"? Nor is there reason to appeal to a tradition phase in Aramaic, since every context in Mark can find adequate explanation on the basis of the Greek text. And so, the editorial literary history of this "discourse" of Jesus cannot reach further than Mark who has assembled a number of loose sayings of Jesus.[7] One can suspect some editorial intervention in the formulation in v. 50 (the conclusion), as well as in vv. 33-34 and 36 which introduce the sayings and can in any case stand by themselves (cf. Mk. 10, 43-44; Mt. 10, 40; Lk. 10, 16). Yet it would not be wise to exclude all prehistory. The close parallels in the sayings about scandal of hand, foot and eye (vv. 43, 45, 47) constitute a small group in which one can sense the rhythm of the spoken word. It is perhaps the primitive nucleus which was expanded, on the one hand, with an introduction—the saying about the scandal given to the little ones (not the "subjective" scandal of a part of one's own body)—and, on the other, at the end with the addition of the sayings about fire and salt (vv. 42-50). With this we have anticipated the examination of the parallels in Matthew and Luke.

MATTHEW 18, 1-4

It is easy to understand that Matthew was not satisfied with the composition of Mark 9, 33-37. The disciples' quarrel about precedence is answered there with the saying about being the last and the servant (vv. 33-35), but the connection with the following verses (36-37) is, to say the least, somewhat obscure. Matthew worked both elements into a closely knit whole. In a stock introduction the disciples phrased the question in direct speech (v. 1), and Jesus' answer corresponds in strictly verbal order (v. 4). Mark's words, from "who was the greatest" to "servant of all", are followed in Matthew by a saying which Luke

[7] Cf. vv. 33-35, 36-37, 38-39, 40, 41, 42, 43-45, 47, 48, 49, 50a and 50b.

also has made use of in two places (14, 11 and 18, 14). In both 23, 11-12 and 18, 4 Matthew makes this connection, each time with his own formula: "Whoever humbles himself. . . ." The detached scene with the child is incorporated in the conversation. In Mark we should perhaps think of an orphan, in view of the saying about "receiving" in v. 37, but Matthew links it with the blessing of the children in Mark 10, 13-16.[8] Mark 10, 15 is picked up in 18, 3 and gives the main thought of this short pericope: "like children" and "like this child". In Matthew the small child symbolizes the *disposition of the Christian who must become like a child:* the kingdom of heaven belongs to the poor in spirit (cf. 5, 3).

MATTHEW 18, 5-6

In the analysis of Mark, I have pointed out that 9, 42 links up with v. 37: "one such child", "one of these little ones". Matthew goes further and makes both verses follow each other: "he who receives", "he who causes to sin" (18, 5-6). Vv. 1-4 dealt with a real child, a symbol of the spiritual lowliness of the Christian. Some want to extend this sense to "one of these children" in v. 5, but after vv. 3-4 "such a child" is rather the Christian who has become like a child. The parallel of 10, 40 is of a formal character: "whoever receives you". From Mark 9, 37a, Matthew passes over to 9, 42 where there is no doubt about the direct reference to Christians: "he who believes"; Matthew then adds: "in me". This is one of those small divergences that point to an editor with a sense of accuracy, but who at the same time has neglected the close connection with Mark 9, 43-48 (from "it is better" to "to be thrown"; cf. Mt. 18, 8-9).[9] Whoever causes the little ones to sin is threatened with a curse. The abridged version of Mark 9, 37 in v. 5 can be understood as a parallel: "he who receives such a child receives me." In the light

[8] Cf. 9, 36 and 10, 16: "embracing"; 9, 37 and 10, 15: "receiving" of the child, of the kingdom of God *like* a child.

[9] Namely, "in me" (cf. 27-42: "in him"), "it is better that" (cf. 5, 29-30; 19, 10), "suspending", "drowning" (cf. 14, 30), "into the depth".

of 25, 34-40 we may see in this a promise of reward. Thus Matthew remains faithful to Mark's composition where the saying about scandal is preceded by v. 41 which is a clear commentary on the saying of v. 37 in this sense.

Compared with Mark (cf. Luke 17, 1b) Matthew 18, 7 is new. It is hardly strange that Matthew brought together sayings about "causing to sin" from Mark and Q. He even uses "conflation" of the two sources (i.e., bringing together into smaller compass); 12, 31-32 and 13, 31-32 are perhaps the clearest examples of this. But in our case it is not really a matter of conflation (or condensed duplicate). Luke 17, 1-2 is often quoted without further qualification as a text of the twofold tradition on which Matthew 18, 6-7 would depend (with a reversal of the order of the sayings). But Luke 17, 2 shows no specific similarity with Matthew 18, 6, and negative agreements against Mark ("it is better" and "to be thrown") only confirm that Mark 9, 42 has been handled in two independent ways. The introductory verse (1a: "he said to them") betrays the hand of the evangelist. For the connection of Mark 9, 42 with 1b (Q) he may have been inspired by the word about the traitor in Mark 14, 21. The scheme is identical: "it is necessary (as it is written)"—"woe to him who"—"it would be better for him". Whichever way one looks at it, it is difficult to see in 17, 1-2 a primitive connection because v. 2b gives these verses a clearly edited character; the words "than that he should cause to sin" limp lamely at the end and have been pushed out of their proper place by v. 1c. Thus Matthew and Luke both linked, each in his own way, the saying of Mark 9, 42 with the apocalyptic saying from Q about the inevitability of scandal. Matthew did this with an editorial transition with which I must still deal (v. 7a).

MATTHEW 18, 7-9

Matthew 18, 8-9 (parallel with Mark 9, 43. 45. 47) was, according to many authors, influenced by the two verses of 5, 29-30, derived from the twofold tradition. In Butler's view it is a repetition of 5, 29-30 and at the same time the source of Mark. This needs straightening out. Mark's trilogy of hand, foot and eye is in both versions of Matthew a double saying, introduced each time by "if" with the indicative and an identical mention of the cutting off, plucking out and throwing off of members of the body. The agreements are undeniable but are they more than a mere parallel reaction of the same editor to Mark's text? In the Sermon on the Mount, 5, 29-30 was added to the antithesis about adulterous lust. After the statement about the lustful look, the words about the eye obviously come first.[10] In Matthew's description of the maiming, one can see a closer paraphrase of Mark: "cutting off", "plucking out" (*ekbale*) (Mk.)—"plucking out", "cutting off", "throwing away" (*bale apo sou*) (Mt. 5 and 18). With the "throwing" and "going into hell", Matthew 5, 29-30 follows Mark literally. Matthew 18, 8-9 combines hand and foot in one saying, but for the rest it follows Mark closely with a few explainable differences: "it is better for you" (the dative is the more usual form), to enter *life* (parallel with v. 8), the hell of *fire* (sums up Mk. 9, 48).

By themselves the sayings undoubtedly deal with the scandal man creates for himself. According to their original meaning we can say in any case that they point to the great sacrifices for which man must be prepared in order "to enter life". In this primitive sense Matthew applies them to sexual sins (5, 29-30). In Matthew 18 we have a different context. One may ask whether the sayings were not already suited to that context in Mark and so understood as a warning against causing others to sin. Yet Matthew 18, 7 suggests another modification. Perhaps we must understand the "scandals" of the editorial verse (7a) in a personal sense (cf. especially 13, 41; 16, 23; 24, 10-12) and link them with the urgent warnings against the false prophets (cf. 7, 15-23). These are the "members" who threaten the community and against whom Christians must protect themselves.

[10] It is not excluded that another saying about the eye (6, 22-23) has influenced the formulation of 5, 29-30: "one of your members—your whole body". Other details: right eye and right hand (cf. 5, 39), "it is better than" (cf. 18, 6).

MATTHEW 18, 10-14

It is time to return to Vaganay's hypothesis, and particularly to what is special to it—namely, the reconstruction of a concatenation of the texts containing "one of these little ones", consisting of Matthew 10, 42 (= Mk. 9, 41); 18, 10; 18, 14; 18, 6 (= Mk. 9, 42). The evangelist would have taken 18, 10. 14 from this in order to provide a framework for the parable of the lost sheep. But it is very doubtful whether these verses ever existed apart from their context. Both parts of Matthew 18 are concluded with a parable, each time with an application introduced by "thus",[11] which picks up the key word of the section: "one of these little ones"—"his brother" (18, 14. 35). Matthew 14 clearly ousts the original conclusion of the parable (cf. v. 13b with Lk. 15, 7). The editor again takes up the saying of 11, 26— borrowed from Q, in his typical terminology—but in the second part of the verse he still shows the influence of the parable— "that one (neuter!) of these little ones should perish" (according to mss. S and B). The surprising neuter (cf. vv. 6 and 10) can be explained with "one (neuter) of them" (v. 12) and the verb may indicate that he knew the parable in Luke's version (three times replaced in Matthew by "getting lost"). The same context may have influenced Matthew 18, 10: the conclusion of the parallel parable of the lost coin (Lk. 15, 10). Matthew 18, 10 is really a transitional verse where the author passes from the theme of "scandal" to that of a positive attitude toward "the little ones". By way of conclusion v. 10 takes up the key word of v. 6. If, finally, we accept with L. Vaganay that the evangelist has transferred Mark 9, 41 to the missionary discourse (10, 42) this may also have been accompanied with a clarification inspired by Mark 9, 42. We may notice *en passant* that Matthew 10, 40-42 is a model of an editorial *linking up through the use of key words*.

[11] Cf. 12, 45b; 13, 40. 49; 20, 16.

LUKE 9, 46-50

Lastly, a word about the editing process in Luke. He, too, is not satisfied with the loose context of Mark. The key word "name" no longer appeals to him (Mk. 9, 39b, a. c.), but in his own way he makes the connection closer by using the verb "answer" (v. 49). He also makes use of Mark 9, 37 in the question of precedence. This makes it difficult to provide a satisfactory explanation of v. 48c (cf. Mk. 9, 35; 10, 43-44; Lk. 22, 44-47; 7, 28). We may hold on to this: in the humbleness of the service to this child lies the greatness of the disciples. Thematically, too, Luke 9, 46-50 constitutes a whole: quarrelsomeness and jealousy among the disciples of Jesus ("of them", "among you all") and toward strangers ("with us", "against you", "for you"). Here the perspective is more historical and less directly catechetical than in Matthew 18.

Insofar as omissions are concerned, we are, as usual, reduced to guessing. Matthew left out Mark 9, 38-39. Why? Because of the reproach of the disciple whom he wants to spare? Because he has already used these verses in 7, 22? Because he found them less useful to give the concrete presentation he wanted to provide in Matthew 18? In regard to the omission of Mark 9, 42-50 in Luke, one could consider the abridging tendency with an eye on the narrative of the journey, or that Luke might have been afraid of duplicating, or that he wanted to avoid terms that were too harsh or too brutal. There may also have been the influence of association here with the same effect as it has in connection with a key word. The Samaritans of 9, 51-56 do not "receive" Jesus (cf. v. 48). John and James react in a way which draws a rebuke (cf. vv. 49-50).

TRANSMITTING AND EDITING

These rather summary reflections no doubt require comparison with other ways of approaching the problem. Although I cannot indulge in that here, it may already have become clear that the versions of Matthew and Luke may be understood as "improvements" and adaptations of Mark, which, however, throw little light on the prehistory of Mark 9, 33-50. It is true that we have parallels and duplications of individual sayings: for v. 35 (Mk. 10, 43-44; 10, 31); v. 37 (Lk. 10, 16 = Mt. 10, 40); v. 40 (Mt. 12, 30); v. 50 (Lk. 13, 34-35 = Mt. 5, 13). I have doubts about Matthew 10, 42 for v. 41 and Luke 17, 1-2 for v. 42. But for the mutual connection between the sayings we lack positive indications of a pre-Mark tradition. The straightforward key-word connections of vv. 42-50 provide the first approach here. It is somewhat different for vv. 33-41. There is obviously a connection of vv. 38-39 with v. 37 in the key word "name", but the absence of a conjunction as in v. 38a is by no means unusual in Mark's editing. This "name" is used again in v. 41 (after v. 40, but by way of conclusion, and not as verbal reporting, *ad vocem*), but there is no connection with v. 42. This allows us to suspect that, in their own way, both these verses refer to v. 37: a procedure of editorial composition, and not the key-word connection of an oral transmission. Would an Aramaic version help us any further? Perhaps on one point: namely, the connection between vv. 35 and 36-37, with the help of the *key word* "talya" in "servant"/"child". On the other hand, the word "servant" would more usually refer to "abda" and the diversity of the parallel situations (10, 42-45 and 10, 13-16 respectively) does not point to a very close connection of v. 35 with vv. 36-37. Therefore, on this point, too, we cannot lightly ignore the contribution of the evangelist himself.

Joseph Fitzmyer, S.J./*Woodstock, Md.*

The Son of David Tradition and Matthew 22, 41-46 and Parallels

Any discussion of the development of tradition in its relation to scripture should cope with examples of this relation in scripture itself. The problem of scripture and tradition in the Christian Church developed in its own way once the canon of the New Testament was fixed. But there is a relationship between these realities manifest in the New Testament itself, particularly as Old Testament traditions are taken up and adapted to the formation of later scriptures. Even if such New Testament examples are not in every respect comparable to instances of the later development of Christian doctrine, nevertheless they have facets which merit a renewed consideration for the light they shed on the contemporary problem.

One passage which lends itself readily to such a consideration is the debate about the Messiah as the son of David in Mt. 22, 41-46 and its parallels (Mk. 12, 35-37a; Lk. 20, 41-44). The figure of the Davidic Messiah expected in Judaism about the time of Christ was the product of a long tradition. However complicated its previous history was, it receives a significant interpretation in the synoptics. We turn then to this episode as an example of an evolving tradition rooted in the Old Testament motif of the son of David.

Mt. 22, 41-46	Mk. 12, 35-37a	Lk. 20, 41-44
⁴¹"Now when the Pharisees were gathered together, Jesus asked them a question, ⁴²saying, "What do you think of the Messiah? Whose son is he?" They said to him, "The son of David." ⁴³He said to them, "How is it then that David, inspired by the Spirit, calls him Lord, saying,	³⁵And as Jesus taught in the temple, he said, "How can the scribes say that the Messiah	⁴¹But he said to them, "How can they say that the Messiah is
	the son of David?	the son of David?
	³⁶David himself, inspired by the Holy Spirit, declared,	⁴²For David himself says in the Book of Psalms,
⁴⁴'The Lord said to my Lord, Sit at my right hand, till I put your enemies under your feet? ⁴⁵If David thus calls him Lord, how is he his son?" ⁴⁶And no one was able to answer him a word, nor from that day did anyone dare to ask him any more questions.	The Lord said to my Lord, Sit at my right hand, till I put your enemies under your feet. ³⁷David himself calls him Lord; so how is he his son?"	The Lord said to my Lord, Sit at my right hand,⁴³till I make your enemies a stool for your feet.' ⁴⁴David thus calls him Lord; so how is he his son?"

This pericope forms part of the synoptic account of the last days of Jesus in Jerusalem. In its earliest form (Mk. 12) the passage records a dominical saying, "As Jesus taught in the temple, he said. . . ." In Mark there is scarcely any evidence of debate, and the setting is hardly different in Luke. But in Matthew 22 the Gospel tradition has clothed the saying with controversy so that it rather resembles an apophthegm.[1] In any setting the substance of the saying is the same: Jesus questions the contemporary tradition about the Messiah as the son of David, implying that the Davidic Messiah must be understood in some other way. Among others, R. Bultmann believes that not Jesus himself but the early Church made this identification

[1] R. Bultmann, The History of the Synoptic Tradition (New York, 1963), pp. 51, 137, 405 (Ger. ed.: Die Geschichte der synoptischen Tradition).

of Jesus and the son of David.[2] But V. Taylor has effectively shown that this saying cannot be wholly due to a community formulation, since the allusive character of the saying, half-concealing and half-revealing the "messianic secret", is difficult to explain as the doctrinal belief of a community. It stands in contrast to the tone and frankness of such passages as Acts 2, 34-36; 5, 31; 10, 42-43; Rom. 1, 2-4; etc.[3]

Before asking in what sense the saying is to be understood, we must review the prior tradition about David.

The David Tradition in the Old Testament

Within the Old Testament itself the David tradition apparently grew up independently of Israel's ancient *credo* derived from the early period of its salvation history. Only with the passage of time were the two traditions fused; this occurred about the time of the exile in such writers as Ezekiel, Second Isaiah, Haggai, Zechariah and Nehemiah. Yahweh's intervention on behalf of David was at that time seen to be a continuation of the salvific deeds recalled in Israel's ancient *credo*.

The earliest tradition about David is embedded in the work of the Deuteronomist and concerns David's role in the story of the ark of the covenant (1 Sam. 4, 1—7, 1; 2 Sam. 6, 1-15. 17-20a), his accession to the throne (1 Sam. 16, 1-2; 2 Sam. 5, 25; 6, 16. 20b-23; 9, 1-13), his dynasty (2 Sam. 7, 1-29; 11, 2-20. 26; 1 Kg. 1, 1-2. 46) and his last words (2 Sam. 23, 1-7). At this stage David is depicted as the zealous worshiper of Yahweh (2 Sam. 6, 6-9), "chosen" by him to rule over all Israel in place of Saul (2 Sam. 6, 21), and favored by his Word (1 Sam. 25, 31; 2 Sam. 3, 9-10; 5, 2). David is the obedient

[2] R. Bultmann, *Theology of the New Testament*, I (London, 1956), p. 28. Cf. also E. Klostermann, *Das Markusevangelium* (Handbuch zum Neuen Testament, 3) (Tübingen, [4]1950), p. 129; B. H. Branscomb, *The Gospel of Mark* (Moffatt New Testament Commentary) (London, 1937), pp. 222-25.

[3] V. Taylor, *The Gospel according to St. Mark* (London, 1953), p. 493. Cf. also R. P. Gagg, "Jesus und die Davidssohnfrage: Zur Exegese von Markus 12, 35-37," in *Theol. Zeitschrift* 7 (1951), pp. 18-30; O. Cullmann, *The Christology of the New Testament* ([2]1963), p. 132.

servant whose respect for Yahweh is shown in his slaying of the Amalekite who raised his hand against Saul, Yahweh's anointed. Yet Yahweh has not favored David for himself alone; David is to rule over Israel and his kingly role affects all Israel. Yahweh's choice of David is, therefore, an event of corporate salvific significance for the history of Israel.[4]

Two passages in particular stress this aspect of David's role: the oracle of Nathan (2 Sam. 7, 14-17) and the "last words of David" (2 Sam. 23, 1-17). Nathan makes it clear that Yahweh's favor is not limited to David himself: "When your days are fulfilled and you lie down with your fathers, I will raise up after you your offspring who shall come forth from your body; and I will establish its kingdom. He shall build a house for my name and I will establish his royal throne forever. I will be his father and he shall be my son" (2 Sam. 7, 12-14). The significance of this oracle is seen in David's "last words" in which the psalmist of Israel is hailed as "the anointed of the God of Jacob" (2 Sam. 23, 1). David is explicitly called $m\bar{a}\check{s}\hat{i}^{a}h$, an anointed agent of Yahweh. The oracle is a "covenant" made by Yahweh with the Davidic dynasty: "For Yahweh has made with me an everlasting covenant" (23, 5). The Davidic tradition is now framed in covenantal terms, and it rivals, as it were, the ancient covenant of Sinai. It thus gives Israel's traditions a new center of gravity.

This basic tradition about David underwent development in the royal psalms, in the prophets and in post-exilic writings. In the psalms which mention David (Pss. 18, 72, 89, 132, 144) his title of "anointed" is explicitly repeated (Pss. 18, 51; 89, 39. 52 [cf. v. 20]; 132, 10. 17). Psalm 132, 2 ascribes to him a more prominent role in the building of the temple; he is said to have made a *vow* to build it. Yahweh's promise in the oracle of Nathan becomes a divine *oath* (Pss. 132, 11; 89, 4. 36-37. 50). But above all these psalms stress the enduring and unshak-

---

[4] Cf. S. Mowinckel, *He That Cometh* (Oxford, 1956); S. Amsler, *David, roi et messie* (Cahiers théologiques, 49) (Neuchâtel, 1963); R. A. Carlson, *David, the Chosen King* (Stockholm, 1964).

able character of the Davidic dynasty (Pss. 18, 51; 89, 5. 30. 37; 132, 10-12). It will last forever, and the very cultic hymns of the psalter attest to its continuance. Psalm 2, a royal psalm which does not mention David, promises universal dominion to a Davidic king. The king is Yahweh's "anointed", indeed his very son: "You are my son; today I have begotten you" (2, 7). Another royal psalm, probably composed for the enthronement of some Davidic king, depicts him as one invited by Yahweh to sit at his right hand and to share his exalted heavenly glory: "The Lord says to my lord, 'Sit at my right hand, till I make your enemies your footstool' " (Ps. 110, 1). Thus an intimate relationship between Yahweh and the anointed Davidic heir is established.

The continuance of the Davidic dynasty is assured at the time of the Syro-Ephraimite war as Isaiah announces to Ahaz, in a moment of impending doom, the birth of a royal heir; "a child" is to be born who will be a "wonderful counselor, mighty God, everlasting Father, Prince of peace", and will sit "upon the throne of David" (Is. 9, 6-7). He will be "a shoot from the stump of Jesse" (11, 1). To Hezekiah the prophet eventually announces Yahweh's further message: "I will defend this city to save it, for my own sake and for the sake of my servant David" (37, 35).

As Jeremiah confronted the last of the Davidic kings before Nebuchadnezzar's invasion, he called Israel to a renewed fidelity to its ancient *credo*. But he juxtaposed to this appeal allusions to the Davidic tradition. He announced that the Davidic king Jehoiakim would "have none [i.e., no heir] to sit upon the throne of David" (Jer. 36, 30); and yet the same prophet uttered the promise of a "new covenant" and proclaimed that the people of Israel would "serve Yahweh their God and David their king, whom I will raise up for them" (30, 9).

In Jeremiah's words there is a significant development, for "David" is now regarded as a future occupant of the throne to be raised up by Yahweh. The ideal king will be a "David". "Days are coming, says the Lord, when I will raise up for David a righteous branch; he shall reign as king and deal wisely and shall execute justice and righteousness in the land" (Jer. 23, 5). Salvation, justice and righteousness are the qualities linked with the reign of the new son of David. Ezekiel's message is similarly reassuring in the wake of the destruction of Jerusalem: "They shall be my people and I will be their God; my servant David shall be king over them and they shall all have one shepherd" (Ezek. 37, 23-24).

Significant in this prophetic development of a future sense of "David" is the complete absence of the title *māšiᵃḥ*. The word occurs but twice in the prophets: once applied to Cyrus (Is. 45, 1) and once to the king or the nation (Hab. 3, 13). The prophets indeed echo the oracle of Nathan in some sense. But even though David was clearly hailed earlier as Yahweh's "anointed", they significantly do not speak of the "coming of a Messiah". They only announce the hope of a restored kingdom of David because Yahweh has promised it.

In post-exilic times the David tradition develops still further. A king no longer rules in Jerusalem, for foreign domination prevents this. Yet the Davidic lineage continues in Zerubbabel, the governor of Judah, who has been "chosen" by Yahweh (Hag. 2, 23; cf. Zech. 6, 12-14). The significant post-exilic development of the David tradition is seen in the chronicler's work. Here the portrait of David is not only idealized, but the account of his reign is schematized. Though 1 Chr. opens with genealogies beginning with Adam, the real history of Israel starts with the death of Saul and the accession of David (1 Chr. 10). The chronicler aims to depict what the ideal kingdom of Israel under God should be like, and he idyllically describes the reigns of David and Solomon not as they were but as they should have been. David is idealized and becomes the real founder of the temple and its cult. The perpetuity of David's reign is stressed (1 Chr. 28, 4).

In this connection the chronicler's modifications of the oracle of Nathan are significant:

2 Sam. 7, 12. 16	1 Chr. 7, 11. 14
I will raise up after you your off-spring who shall come forth from your body. . . . Your house and your kingdom shall be made sure before me forever; your throne shall be established forever.	I will raise up after you your off-spring, who shall be one of your own sons. . . . I will confirm him in my house and in my kingdom forever, and his throne shall be established forever.

Whereas in 2 Samuel "your offspring" (*zar°kā*) was used in a collective sense, the chronicler employs it to refer to a particular descendant in the Davidic line ('*°ser yihyeh mibbānêka*: literally, "who shall be from among your sons"). Again: "I will confirm *him* in *my* house and in *my* kingdom forever," a significant change from the original oracle. The shift makes it clear that a Davidic king to come will be Yahweh's representative in the restored Israelite theocracy. But once again we note the absence of the title *māšî°ḥ* for the Davidic king. If David himself is so named in 2 Chr. 6, 42, this refers to the historic David, not to the expected ideal Davidic ruler.

Finally, only in the 2nd-century B.C. apocalypse of Daniel is there explicit mention of an expected "anointed prince" in Jerusalem: ". . . from the going forth of the Word to restore and build Jerusalem to [the coming of] an anointed one, a prince, there shall be seven weeks" (Dan. 9, 25: *'ad māšî°ḥ nāgîd*). Who is this anointed prince or "Messiah"? A son of David? Probably. Yet this occurrence of the word in Daniel is part of a larger, complex picture of messianic expectations which emerge in the 2nd century B.C.

The Davidic Messiah in Later Judaism

That Daniel 9, 25-26 nourished the Jewish hopes of a restored kingdom of God under the leadership of an ideal king, even called "the Messiah", can be seen in the literature of Qumran. 1QS 9, 11 clearly alludes to Daniel 9, 25, "until the coming of a prophet and the Messiahs of Aaron and Israel".[5] Both the

[5] 1QS = the "rule of the community" of Qumran Cave I; 1QSa = the "rule of the congregation" [= 1Q28a; cf. *infra*, footnote 10]; CD = Damascus Document; 4QPatrBless = Patriarchal Blessings of Qumran Cave IV; 4QpIs° = the first commentary on Isaiah from Qumran Cave

Danielic text and the Qumran literature reflect this stage in the development of Jewish beliefs when it is legitimate to speak of the coming of "a [or the] Messiah", or even of "the Messiahs". Granted that one should beware of reading into these terms all the connotations of New Testament christology, it would be hypocritical to insist at this stage that one should simply speak of "anointed ones".[6] It is precisely these texts which show that a genuine Old Testament theme of an anointed agent of Yahweh had developed into the expectation of a Messiah—and, in the specific case in which we are interested, of a Davidic Messiah. (The expected prophet and the priestly Messiah, or Messiah of Aaron, do not concern us here.)

In the Qumran literature the Davidic Messiah is called the "Messiah of Israel" (1QSa 2, 14. 20; cf. 1QS 9, 11; CD 20, 1). In 4QPatrBless. 2, 4 (a sort of commentary on Gen. 49, 10) we read of the coming of "the Messiah of righteousness, the shoot of David" ('d bw' mšyḥ hṣdq ṣmḥ dwyd), for to him and to his seed has been given the royal mandate over his people for everlasting generations.[7] Important too is the interpretation of the oracle of Nathan in 4QFlorilegium 1, 11-13.[8] Having quoted 2 Samuel 7, 11-14 in abbreviated form, the author comments: "This is the shoot of David who is to arise with the interpreter of the Law who [will arise] in Zi[on in the l]ast days; as it is written, *And I will raise up the booth of David that is fallen. That is the booth of David which is fall[en and after]ward he will arise to save Israel.*" A salvific mission is thus clearly associated with the Davidic Messiah. One could also cite 4QpIs[a] D, 1-5, which relates Isaiah 11, 1 to the "shoot of David", and 4QTestimonia 9-13, which applies the oracle of Balaam (Num. 24, 15-17) to the Davidic Messiah.[9] (Cf. also Enoch 48, 10; 52, 4.)

IV. For a bibliography on Qumran Messianism, cf. my article in *Cath. Bibl. Quarterly* 27 (1965), pp. 349-50, footnote 7.

[6] Cf. J. Carmignac, *Les textes de Qumran*, II (Paris, 1963), p. 13; L. Silbermann, "The Two Messiahs of the Manual of Discipline," in *Vetus Testamentum* 5 (1955), pp. 77-82; M. Smith, "What Is Implied by the Variety of Messianic Figures?" in *Journ. Bibl. Lit.* 78 (1959), pp. 66-72.

[7] Cf. J. M. Allegro, *Journ. Bibl. Lit.* 75 (1956), pp. 174-75.

[8] Cf. *Journ. Bibl. Lit.* 77 (1958), p. 353.

[9] Cf. *Journ. Bibl. Lit.* 75 (1956), pp. 180-81, 183-84.

Qumran literature thus attests the full flowering of an Old Testament tradition about David. The title *māšiᵃḥ* is given to an ideal son of David, expected in the "end of days". Elements of that belief, sown like seeds in the Old Testament, gradually grew and matured into an extrabiblical tradition intimately associated with the biblical books. Thus far no text has turned up in the Qumran caves giving this future Davidic Messiah the title "Son of God", although it is possible that one text speaks of God "begetting the Messiah" (1QSa 2, 11-12).[10] Again, no text yet applies to him the words of Psalm 2, 7 or the words of Psalm 110.

Outside of Qumran but still in pre-Christian times the expectation of a son of David as a Messiah is also attested in the (probably pharisaic) *Psalms of Solomon:* "Raise up, O Lord, unto them their king, the son of David . . . that he may reign over Israel thy servant. . . . There shall be no unrighteousness in their midst in his days, for all shall be holy and their king the anointed of the Lord" (17, 23. 36; cf. 18, 6. 8).[11] This expectation is echoed in the later rabbinical tradition. Though we can never be sure how early the elements of this rabbinical tradition are, it is at least a legitimate continuation of an understanding of the David tradition well attested among the Jews of Palestine in pre-Christian times.[12]

The Son of David Question in the Synoptics

Against the background of such a tradition and its development the words of Jesus in Matthew 22, 41-46 must now be judged. In conversation with the Pharisees Jesus raises a question

---

[10] Cf. D. Barthélemy and J. T. Milik, *Qumran Cave I* (Discoveries in the Judean Desert, 1) (Oxford, 1955), pp. 110, 117. On the problem of the reading, cf. my remarks in *Cath. Bibl. Quarterly* 27 (1965), p. 367.

[11] In this text we meet for the first time the title "son of David" used in connection with the expectations of the Palestinian Jews. Cf. also E. Lohse, "Der König aus Davids Geschlecht: Bemerkungen zur messianischen Erwartung der Synogoge," in *Abraham unser Vater: Juden und Christen im Gespräch über die Bibel: Festschrift für Otto Michel* (Leiden, 1963), pp. 337-45.

[12] In this regard one could cite the Targum on the prophets to Isaiah 11, 1; Midrash Psalm 18, 36; Psalm 21, 1. Cf. also H. L. Strack and P. Billerbeck, *Kommentar zum Neuen Testament*, IV (Munich, 1928), pp. 452-65.

about the Davidic origin of the Messiah.[13] Having posed it, he raises the problem of Psalm 110: How could David, the reputed and inspired author of that psalm, be the father of the messianic king whom he calls "Lord"? "The Lord [*Yahweh, Kyrios*] said to my lord (*la' ᵃdōnî, tô kyriô mou* [= the anointed king]), 'Sit at my right hand. . . .' "

The explanation of this saying of Jesus is not easy and has taken various forms in the history of its exegesis. We single out three general interpretations. (1) J. Klausner and others have thought that Jesus' argumentation implies that he is calling in question the Davidic origin of the Messiah. "Jesus had already declared himself Messiah. But the Messiah was to be the *son of David,* whereas Jesus was a Galilean and the son of Joseph the carpenter! How could he be the Messiah? To evade this serious difficulty Jesus must find a passage of scripture according to which the Messiah need not necessarily be the son of David, and like an expert pharisee he finds it." [14] (2) Many ancient and modern commentators have understood his question to imply that the Messiah is something more than a mere son of David, having a more exalted, transcendent origin than David, seeing that the latter calls him "Lord". Jesus would thereby insinuate a secret about himself, but no further specification is made in the text.[15] (3) J. Schniewind and others press beyond the second interpretation in specifying that Jesus is in fact referring to the vision of the "Son of Man" in Daniel 7, 13. Jesus is indeed the son of David, but he is more; he is the Son of Man in a unique sense.[16]

---

[13] One might be tempted to think that the question arose out of the Essene belief in two Messiahs, one of Aaron, the other of Israel. However, there is no evidence that such a background to the question was responsible here. The problem is wholly concerned with the Davidic Messiah.

[14] J. Klausner, *Jesus of Nazareth: His Life, Times, and Teaching* (New York, 1926), p. 320. Cf. also C. G. Montefiore, *The Synoptic Gospels,* I (London, 1909), pp. 290-92.

[15] Cf., for example, V. Taylor, *op. cit.,* p. 492; A. H. McNeill, *The Gospel according to St. Matthew* (London, 1915), p. 328.

[16] J. Schniewind, *Das Evangelium nach Markus* (Das Neuen Testament Deutsch, 1) (Göttingen, ¹⁰1963), pp. 164-65. Cf. P. Bonnard, *L'évangile selon saint Matthieu* (Commentaire de Nouveau Testament, 1) (Neuchâtel, 1963), pp. 330-31.

Regarding these interpretations several points should be noted. The first explanation is generally abandoned because it is inexplicable how Jesus would have intended to attack a well-founded belief in the Davidic origin of the Messiah (cf. *supra* for the Old Testament texts). The New Testament gives no evidence of such an intention; indeed, such a denial of the scriptures would have given his opponents ground for the charge against him (cf. Jn. 8, 5). Again, it is really farfetched to maintain that Jesus did not know he was of Davidic lineage.[17] An early level of New Testament tradition attests it (Rom. 1, 3), and ostensibly without any apologetic intent. It is also echoed in later levels (Mk. 10, 47-48; Mt. 1, 1; Lk. 3, 31; 2 Tim. 2, 8). Would not Jesus' denial of the Davidic origin of the Messiah have left some other trace, in view of the New Testament stress on his role as one who fulfilled the Old Testament?

The real choice lies today between the second and the third explanations. Here I think a distinction must be made. It is not unlikely that the evangelists, especially Matthew with his secondary additions to the episode, were implying something like the third explanation in recording it.[18] But the question is legitimately asked whether Jesus himself, in the original *Sitz im Leben* of the incident, implied all that the early Church understood by it in the light of its Easter and Pentecostal faith.

It is not impossible that the synoptic accounts of this episode represent only a torso of the full account. Since the rest of the dialogue resembles similar altercations with pharisees (cf. Mk. 2, 9. 17-19; 3, 4), it may be that it was they who asked the first question, something like: "You too teach, don't you, that the Messiah is David's son?" And rather than answer it with "yes" or "no", Jesus posed a counter-question (cf. Mt. 22, 17). Jesus' answer then would have had the form of a scribal debate, aimed more at meeting the pharisees on the level of haggadic scriptural

[17] Cf. W. Michaelis, "Die Davidssohnschaft Jesu als historisches und kerygmatisches Problem," in *Der historische Jesus und der kerygmatische Christus*, eds. H. Ristow and K. Matthiae (Berlin, ²1961), pp. 317-30, esp. pp. 321-24.

[18] *Ibid.*, pp. 318-19; cf. B. M. F. van Iersel, *"Der Sohn" in den synoptischen Jesusworten* (Supplements to Novum Testamentum, 3) (Leiden, 1964), pp. 171-73.

interpretation than of suggesting that he was personally of some other than Davidic origin.[19] The question is one of emphasis, for the latter aspect cannot be fully excluded.

The background of such debate has been plausibly suggested by D. Daube, who has noted in Matthew 22 four types of exegetical questions often also grouped together in rabbinical tradition.[20] There are the pharisees' question about tribute to Caesar (15-22), the Sadducees' question about levirate marriage and the resurrection (23-33), the pharisees' question about the great commandment of the Law (34-40), and, finally, the pharisees' question about the Messiah, son of David (41-46). These questions correspond respectively to the rabbinical grouping of four questions concerning hokmāh ("wisdom": i.e., halakic interpretation of legal texts), bōrût (vulgarity": i.e., questions designed to ridicule a belief), derek 'ereṣ ("way of the land": i.e., the principle of moral conduct) and haggadāh ("legend": i.e., the interpretation of biblical passages with apparent contradictions). In this case, Jesus would be propounding a haggadāh question arising from the contradiction of the Messiah as David's son and David's Lord. It implies that both ideas are correct: the Messiah is David's son (in his earthly appearance), but also David's Lord.[21] We cannot be certain about this because the passage is so cryptic. It is not impossible that he also implied in his answer that the Messiah was therefore less involved politically than the common belief depicted him to be.[22]

At any rate, a more developed stage of the son of David tradition developed with the writing of the synoptic gospels. As the evangelists incorporated this episode into their gospels, it was almost certainly with a view to exploiting the nuances of the title kyrios and applying to Jesus the Messiah the words of

[19] Cf. R. P. Gagg, op. cit., pp. 24-29. We would not necessarily agree with all the individual details of this article.

[20] D. Daube, The New Testament and Rabbinic Judaism (London, 1956), pp. 158-63. In quoting Daube, we do not mean to imply that he equates this four-question structure with Jesus' ministry itself; it may be due to the evangelists, as he suggests.

[21] Cf. J. Jeremias, Jesus' Promise to the Nations (Studies in Biblical Theology, 24) (Naperville, Ill., 1958), p. 53.

[22] Cf. O. Cullmann, op. cit., pp. 132-33.

Psalm 110, 1. By that time *kyrios,* used of Jesus, carried with it the clear suggestion that he was somehow on a par with Yahweh of the Old Testament. Moreover, the use of Psalm 110, 1 elsewhere in the New Testament clearly emphasizes Jesus' exaltation to lordship and heavenly glory (cf. Mk. 16, 19; 1 Cor. 15, 25; Eph. 1, 20; Col. 3, 1; Heb. 8, 1; 10, 12-13; 12, 2), and at times stands in contrast to his Davidic relationship (Acts 2, 29-35; 13, 23-39; Heb. 1, 3-13).[23]

In this regard three things should be noted: (1) It is highly questionable that the Davidic Messiah was given the title of Son of Man in pre-Christian times.[24] It is unlikely therefore that Jesus himself was referring to a well-known identification of the Messiah in his cryptic question. (2) The disciples, as depicted in the earliest gospel strata, apparently did not make this equation during the earthly ministry of Jesus.[25] (3) Even though Psalm 110 has no clear reference to the Son of Man or, most likely, even to the ideal and expected Davidic Messiah, these links are plausibly traced to Jesus himself. The allusion to Psalm 110 in the trial scene (Mt. 26, 64) suggests this and undoubtedly should be regarded as the springboard for the further development of the son of David tradition in the synoptics. The term of this development, climaxing in Jesus' glorious exaltation and divine sonship, receives explicit formulation in *Ep. Barnabae* 12, 10, when Psalm 110, 1 is quoted in support of the belief that Jesus was "not the son of a man, but the Son of God".

Thus the Davidic Messiah is a prime example of a biblical motif which developed in a tradition even extra-biblically attested to, but which was never completely divorced from its biblical roots. It grew and evolved beyond the limits of the Old Testament assertions and received a strong further impetus in Jesus' debate with the pharisees over the Davidic origin of the Messiah.

[23] Cf. E. Lövestamm, "Die Davidssohnfrage," in *Svensk Exegetisk Arsbok* 27 (1962), pp. 72-82.
[24] Cf. H. H. Rowley, "The Suffering Servant and the Davidic Messiah," in *The Servant of the Lord and Other Essays on the Old Testament* (Oxford, ²1965), pp. 82-84.
[25] *Ibid.,* p. 84.

David Stanley, S.J./*Willowdale, Canada*

The Primitive Preaching: The Traditional Schema

The purpose of the present study is to seek to recover—from the speeches in the Acts of the Apostles attributed to Peter (Acts 2, 14-36; 3, 12-26; 4, 8-12; 5, 29-32; 10, 34-43), and from Paul's reported address to the Jews of Pisidian Antioch (Acts 13, 16-41)—the basic structure of the kerygma created by the original apostolic group under Peter's leadership and handed down in tradition by the early Church. That such an authenticated, traditional schema did in fact exist by the time Paul composed his letters in the second half of the 1st century appears to be beyond question. Paul alludes to this apostolic tradition as something received by himself (1 Cor. 15, 1) and possessing a sacred, incontrovertible uniqueness (Gal. 1, 6-7) which had been guaranteed by Peter with the Twelve (Gal. 2, 2-9).

On the other hand, the view of C. H. Dodd—expressed thirty years ago in a celebrated little book which has enjoyed wide acceptance—that the Petrine discourses in Acts consist basically of materials that go back to "the Aramaic-speaking Church at Jerusalem",[1] has been recently challenged by Ernst Haenchen in his monumental commentary on Acts.[2] He prefers the view of

[1] C. H. Dodd, *The Apostolic Preaching and Its Developments* (London, ²1963), p. 20.
[2] E. Haenchen, *Die Apostelgeschichte* (Göttingen, ¹³1961), p. 148.

Martin Dibelius that these sermons are the work of Luke himself, while admitting that the sacred writer did not make them up "out of whole cloth".[3] One of Haenchen's main reasons for his view is the necessary functional role which these discourses play in the structural unity of the whole book[4] and the appositeness with which they fit the varying occasions for which they were composed.[5] Since space does not permit a discussion of the authentically traditional character of these discourses, we shall make our own the fairly common opinion of modern scholars that, if they are indeed compositions by the author of Acts, they contain, in addition to certain Lucan editorial adaptations to a specific situation, genuine reminiscences of a very primitive christology which must go back to the early days of the Church's reflection upon the events which formed the focal point of its Christian faith.[6]

This apostolic kerygma was the fruit of the collective first-hand experience by the Twelve of the principal events of Jesus' public ministry, as well as of his new existence after his resurrection; it constituted the official public testimony to Jesus Christ, which was later to provide the fundamental unity to the entire New Testament literature. As we shall presently have occasion to show, *"the pattern of the kerygma runs right through the New Testament, giving to it, amid all its diversity, a deep essential unity"*.[7] As for the content of the kerygma, it consisted of a well-defined series of happenings, beginning with the ministry of John the Baptist and terminating with the risen Christ's ascension (Acts 1, 21-22). It is with the content of the apostolic preaching, as recorded in the speeches of Acts, that we shall

[3] *Ibid.*, p. 73: "Der Autor hat sie freilich nicht aus dem Blauen gegriffen: das Kerygma von Jesus und der Schriftbeweis speisen die Missionspredigten der Acta. . . ." Cf. also pp. 148f.

[4] *Ibid.*, p. 172: "Man lese einmal die Apg im Zusammenhang, aber ohne ihre Reden. Dann wird man spüren, in wie hohem Grade diese Reden dem Buch sein geistliches Gewicht geben."

[5] *Ibid.*, p. 149.

[6] A. Hunter, *Introducing New Testament Theology* (London, 1957), p. 65. Cf. also the nuanced statement of J. Schmitt, *Jésus ressuscité dans la prédication apostolique* (Paris, 1949), p. 31.

[7] A. Hunter, *op. cit.*, p. 68.

principally concern ourselves here, in order to delineate its basic structure, its christology as evinced by the titles given to our Lord and its use of Old Testament *testimonia*.

I

BASIC STRUCTURE OF THE KERYGMA

The kerygma in a very primary sense constituted a God-given message of hope to a non-Christian world in despair of salvation. God had redeemed mankind supremely and definitively through Jesus' earthly career, a career crowned by his heavenly exaltation. This message of hope was followed by an invitation to make the response of Christian faith, sealed with the acceptance of baptism.

The Message of Hope

The apostolic proclamation of the Good News of salvation—according to the discourses in Acts, with which we are concerned—was structured by two antithetic themes. In the first place, Jesus' death at the hands of the Jews and Romans forms a point of contrast with his glorification by God. Peter's accusation of his former co-religionists (Acts 2, 23-24) runs like a refrain through all these speeches: "You did away with him by having him crucified at the hands of pagans. . . . But God raised him. . . ." (cf. Acts 2, 36; 3, 13-15; 4, 10; 5, 30; 10, 39-40; 13, 27-30). Moreover, this polemical note is accentuated by the emotionally colored terms used to designate the death of Jesus (the simple verb "to die", which will become a characteristically Pauline term, never appears!): "to do away with" (Acts 2, 23; 10, 39; 13, 28); "to nail up" (Acts 2, 33); "to crucify" (Acts 2, 36; 4, 10); "to kill" (Acts 3, 15); "to murder" (Acts 5, 30); "to hang up" (Acts 5, 30; 10, 39). We should also observe that attention appears to be directed more naturally to Jesus' exaltation than to his resurrection, and almost invariably this is attributed to God the Father. "God raised him up" (Acts 2, 32; 3, 26; 5, 30; 13, 33. 37), or "glorified" (Acts 3, 13), or "ex-

alted" (Acts 2, 32; 5, 31) him (cf. also Acts 2, 36). When there
is simply a question of Jesus' resurrection, God is said to raise
him "from death" (Acts 3, 15; 4, 10; 13, 30. 34; cf. the
equivalent phrase in Acts 2, 24) or "the third day" (Acts 10,
40). The fact that the Greek terms for "raise" must be thus
qualified to designate the actual resurrection shows that it was
more normal in the early years to refer to God's *exaltation* of
Jesus. This was perhaps due to the influence upon Christian
terminology of certain Old Testament texts appealed to in the
kerygma, as we shall see shortly.

The second antithesis found in these discourses emphasizes
the contrast between Jesus' state during his earthly career and
his newly acquired status at his glorification. Jesus is first proclaimed as "a man accredited to you by God through miraculous
powers and wonders and signs which God worked through him
among you, as you are well aware" (Acts 2, 22). Peter will
relate to Cornelius the high points of Jesus' public ministry:
how he "began from Galilee after the baptism, which John had
preached"; how "God anointed him with the Holy Spirit and
power"; how he "went about doing good and curing all those
oppressed by the devil, because God was with him"; how the
Twelve actually were "witnesses of everything he did in the country of the Jews and of Jerusalem" (Acts 10, 37-39). The version
of the kerygma ascribed to Paul insists upon Jesus' Davidic
lineage (Acts 13, 23) and upon the Baptist's testimony that
Jesus was a greater man than himself (Acts 13, 25).

Although, from the passages cited, Jesus appears to be presented simply as a man, the announcement of his glorification
leaves no room to doubt that Jesus has now acceded to divine
power. "Exalted now at God's right hand and receiving the
promised Holy Spirit from the Father, he has poured out this
which you see and hear," Peter says on Pentecost (Acts 2, 33).
Indeed, "God has made him Lord and Messiah" (Acts 2, 36);
he "has glorified his servant, Jesus" (Acts 3, 13), and by the
power of the new divine name, *Kyrios,* conferred on Jesus, a
man lame from birth has been healed (Acts 3, 16). Moreover,

it is only through the power of this divine name that salvation can come to mankind (Acts 4, 12), and his disciples obey the Lord Jesus with the obedience due to God himself (Acts 5, 30). "He has commanded us to proclaim him to all the people, and to attest that he is the judge appointed by God of the living and the dead" (Acts 10, 42).

Yet, at this early stage, it would seem that Jesus was expected to enter fully upon his messianic office only at his second coming —a final saving event contingent upon the conversion of the Jews. "Therefore, repent and return to God to have your sins blotted out, in order that times of refreshment may come from the face of the Lord, and he may send Jesus, the Messiah destined for you. Him heaven must hold, until the days of the restoration of all things, of which God spoke in ancient times through the mouth of his holy prophets" (Acts 3, 19-21).

The Invitation to Christian Faith and Baptism

The purpose of the kerygma was to effect a religious reorientation (*metanoia*) of those outside the Church and bring them to make an act of Christian faith, which was then sealed by their acceptance of Christian baptism. "Repent, and let each of you have himself baptized in Jesus Christ's name for the remission of his sins, and you will receive the gift of the Holy Spirit" (Acts 2, 37-38). As I have pointed out elsewhere,[8] the descriptive formula, "baptism in Jesus' name", derived in all probability from the fact that it was accompanied by the neophyte's act of faith in Jesus as Lord, *Kyrios* being the "new name" conferred by the Father upon the glorified Christ (cf. Phil. 2, 9-11). The belief of the apostolic Church in the necessity of baptism as the "seal" of justifying faith may be gathered from Paul's remark about the relationship of circumcision to the faith of Abraham (Rom. 4, 11).

[8] D. Stanley, *The Apostolic Church in the New Testament* (Westminster, 1965), pp. 189-92.

II

PRIMITIVE NATURE OF THE CHRISTOLOGY

From this cursory summary of the contents of the early preaching, the primitive character of its christology will already be evident. There is no mention of the incarnation or of the pre-existence of the Son of God. Indeed, nowhere at this early stage was the title "Son of God" given to Jesus (Paul, it would seem from Acts 9, 20, being one of the first to employ it in his preaching). Nor do we find any *explicit* statement, such as that given in 1 Cor. 15, 3, of the redemptive purpose of Jesus' death or of its vicarious efficacy. Finally, nowhere is any allusion made to the love of God or of Christ for men in effecting this work of redemption. In order to assess precisely the degree of theological understanding of the Christ-event reached at this early stage in the Church's reflection, we shall examine the various titles given to Jesus in these résumés of the kerygma in Acts.

The Servant of God

The application of this title to the exalted Christ is attributed to Peter. "The God of Abraham and Isaac and Jacob, the God of our fathers, has glorified his servant Jesus, whom you handed over. . . ." (Acts 3, 13). Later on, the author of Acts represents the evangelist Philip as basing his version of the kerygma upon the celebrated Deutero-Isaian passage which speaks of the vicarious suffering and death, as well as God's exaltation, of the servant (Is. 52, 13—53, 12). While there seems to be little doubt that the apostolic Church, very early in its theological reflection, found the theme of the suffering and glorified servant of God a most congenial vehicle for expressing the redemptive character of Jesus' death, it may well be, as Acts 3, 13 appears to suggest, that the epithet "servant of God" was first employed solely to designate the exalted Christ. Only at a later stage (exemplified by the formula found in 1 Cor. 15, 3) was it used to denote the vicarious nature of Jesus' death. For it is to be observed that the Petrine discourse employs the servant motif to explain the glorified Christ's presence within the Christian community. "For you, first and foremost, God has raised up his servant and sent him to bless you by converting each of you from your evil ways" (Acts 3, 26).

The Anointed

This title seems to have been closely associated with the preceding one in the primitive Church, as may be seen from the fragment of a very ancient community prayer preserved in Acts 4, 24-30. The Greek form of this term was to provide the familiar name "Christ", while its Hebrew counterpart has furnished the word "Messiah". Its frequent appearance in the apostolic preaching proclaims the Christian belief that Jesus was the divinely-given answer to the messianic hopes of Israel (Acts 2, 36; 3, 18; 10, 36). More specifically, its use indicates that the divine oracle, announced to David by Nathan (2 Sam. 7, 14), was incorporated into the kerygma, which spoke of Jesus' Davidic origin (Acts 13, 23). At the same time, it also proclaimed Jesus as "anointed with the Holy Spirit and power" at his baptism in the Jordan (Acts 10, 37).

In the very early years of the Jewish-Christian community, however, this title may well have been reserved for the parousiac Christ, as one very ancient text, incorporated into Acts 3, 20, seems to suggest. It was at his second coming that the exalted Jesus would enter upon his full messianic function.

The Prophet

This archaic designation of Jesus in the kerygma (Acts 3, 22), which appears to have gradually lost its popularity, undoubtedly took its origin from Deuteronomy 18, 15 where Moses is represented as predicting the coming of another prophet like himself. In late Judaism, there was great speculation about this mysterious eschatological figure, which came to be identified as Elijah *redivivus* (cf. Mal. 3, 1ff.; 4, 5; Sir. 48, 10). Among the evangelists, however, only the author of the fourth gospel reserves this title

THE PRIMITIVE PREACHING: THE TRADITIONAL SCHEMA   95

for Jesus (Jn. 1, 45; cf. v. 21); the Synoptics tend to identify John the Baptist as the prophet of the end-time (Mk. 9, 12-13).

The Lord

While the preceding titles do not suggest the divinity even of the exalted Christ, those which follow do so unequivocally. The name *Kyrios,* or Lord, may be said to form the dividing line. In its Aramaic form, it seems to have been used as an honorific appellation for Jesus during his earthly life: *Mari, Mari* (cf. Mk. 7, 21). Theologically more significant is the liturgical usage in the phrase from the ancient Palestinian communities: *Maran atha* ("Come, our Lord!"), probably a eucharistic acclamation expressing faith in Jesus' divine character (1 Cor. 16, 22; cf. Apoc. 22, 20). Although modern scholars are divided as to whether the title "Lord", applied in the apostolic Church to Christ, actually expressed the Christian belief in his divinity, it is significant that the Septuagint—the Greek version of the Hebrew scriptures made by Alexandrian Jews in the centuries immediately preceding the Christian era—rendered the divine name Yahweh by *Kyrios.* It will be recalled that the text of Joel 3, 5 (LXX): "Everyone who invokes the name of the Lord will be saved," is applied to the invocation of Jesus' divine name (i.e., *Kyrios*). The popular use of Ps. 110, 1 in the kerygma to express the effect of Jesus' exaltation as a sharing in the Father's unique prerogative as universal Lord (he is enthroned at God's right hand) in all probability contributed to the evolution of "Lord" as a divine title for the exalted Christ.

The Universal Judge

Another Old Testament divine function was proclaimed as being conferred upon Christ at his exaltation: "judge of the living and the dead" (Acts 10, 42; cf. 17, 30-31). In the faith of Israel, Yahweh alone held the office of "just judge" (Gen. 18, 25), and his acts of gracious favor toward his people were "judgments". Through this designation of Christ as judge, the early Church could express its belief in his divinity.

The Savior

This title was, in Old Testament terminology, practically synonymous with the preceding: Yahweh as judge saved Israel by vindicating its rights; its victories were Yahweh's "acts of justice" (Jg. 5, 11). The exalted Christ is called savior in the primitive kerygma (Acts 5, 31; 13, 23). The Hellenistic religious world applied the term to Aesculapius, god of medicine; it was also used as a divine name in the emperor cult. The need to employ the epithet "savior" would not have been felt in Aramaic-Christian circles, since it was already contained in his theophoric personal name Yēšua' = "Yahweh is salvation"), and the New Testament provides evidence that the Palestinian faithful were fully conscious of the christological significance of the name "Jesus" (cf. Mt. 1, 21; Lk. 1, 31ff.).

Other Divine Titles

Another title applied to the exalted Christ in the kerygma is a term which can mean "prince", "chief" or "originator". The Greek word is *archegos* (Acts 3, 15; 5, 31). Peter calls Christ "the originator of life" and declares that "God has exalted him at his right hand as prince and savior". The epithet will be taken up later by the author of Hebrews to describe the exalted Christ as the leader of the New Israel (Heb. 2, 10; 12, 2) on the journey to the heavenly Jerusalem.

The kerygma also characterizes Jesus as "the holy and the just one" (Acts 3, 14), titles borrowed from the terminology of Second Isaiah, where however the epithet "Holy One" is reserved for Yahweh himself (Is. 40, 26; 41, 23; 51, 15; 55, 13). The adjective "just" is applied to the servant of God (Is. 53, 11). However, even this title would appear to be predicated properly only of God himself (Is. 45, 21).

III

THE OLD TESTAMENT IN THE KERYGMA

We have already remarked upon the unmistakably polemic note present in the primitive kerygma, expressed by the antith-

esis: "You killed Jesus—God raised him!"—an accusation soft-
ened only by the plea of ignorance (Acts 3, 17; 13, 27). This
would seem to suggest that these summaries in Acts go back to
a period anterior to any clearly conceived soteriological synthesis. However, the redemptive nature of Jesus' death is attributed
to "the determinate will and plan of God" (Acts 2, 23), and it
is articulated at least by a general appeal to "the scriptures"
(Acts 3, 17-18; 13, 27-29).

When we examine the specific Old Testament texts appealed
to in the kerygma, it is interesting to observe that the psalter
appears to have been the favorite source of such *testimonia*. As
Balthasar Fischer has remarked, the Christian liturgical use of
the psalms began only in the late 2nd or early 3rd century "when
the youthful Church, turning its back upon hymns that had been
seriously compromised by Gnostic abuses, redirected its attention to the Bible".[9]

Psalm 16, 10 ("You will not allow your holy one to see cor-
ruption") is offered in proof of the fact that David "foresaw the
resurrection of the Messiah and told of it" (Acts 2, 30-31). The
Petrine kerygma connects this event with Jesus' exaltation as his
accession to the throne of David (v. 30), in fulfillment of the
dynastic oracle uttered by Nathan (2 Sam. 7, 12ff.; Ps. 89, 3-4.
19-37). In the sermon attributed to Paul (Acts 13, 34-39),
Psalm 16, 10 is also related to the divine promise made to David
by citing the allusion to it by Second Isaiah (Is. 55, 3).

Two other psalms were used in conjunction with Psalm 16, 10.
The first of these (Ps. 110, 1) was to become a *locus classicus,*
as the continued citation of it in the New Testament testifies.
"Being exalted at God's right hand and receiving the promised
Holy Spirit from the Father, he has poured out this, which you
both see and hear. For David did not go up to heaven, yet he
himself asserts: 'The Lord said to my lord: Sit at my right hand,
until I place your enemies as a footstool for your feet' " (Acts
2, 33-35). The other psalm was destined to function particularly
in Pauline christology, inasmuch as it contained an allusion to

[9] B. Fischer, "Le Christ dans les psaumes," in *La Maison-Dieu* 18
(1951), p. 88.

the divine sonship of the exalted Christ (Ps. 2, 7). Acts 13, 32-33 employs the verse to describe Jesus' resurrection—in a manner reminiscent of Paul's characterization of it for the Romans—as Christ's constitution as "Son of God in power through the resurrection of the dead" (Rom. 1, 4). It will be recalled that a very ancient Christian community prayer was created as a midrash on Psalm 2 (Acts 4, 27-28), which may well represent one of the earliest Jewish-Christian statements of the redemptive character of Jesus' death.

Psalm 118, 22 also provided a description of the exalted Lord Jesus in the kerygma. "He is himself 'the stone rejected by you the builders, now become the keystone'. Nor is there salvation in any other: for there is no other name under heaven given to men by which you must be saved" (Acts 4, 11-12).

The apostolic preaching, in its attempts to present the redemptive death and resurrection of Christ, also pressed into service the significant figures of Old Testament history, who thus become types of "him who was to come". Jesus' exaltation is the fulfillment of the divine promise to Abraham (Gen. 12, 2; 22, 18) and of the covenant God had made with him (Acts 3, 25). He is the eschatological prophet whom Moses in Deuteronomy 18, 15 promised that God would "raise up"—a term which probably molded Christian theological vocabulary (Acts 3, 22-24). We have already taken cognizance of the Davidic typology, of which such frequent use was made. Finally, the glorified Christ is proclaimed as the exalted servant of God whose praises were sung especially in the fourth Servant Song of Second Isaiah (Acts 3, 13).

IV

The Kerygma and the Unity of the New Testament

While the apostolic kerygma was preached to outsiders in order to convert them to Christianity, it must not be forgotten that basically the same apostolic testimony (insofar as content is concerned) was given within the heart of the Christian community (Acts 2, 42), where "the apostles continually bore witness with great power to the resurrection of the Lord Jesus" (Acts 4, 32). Accordingly, it is not unreasonable to seek in the kerygma the key to the unity of the entire New Testament. "Whatever the literary form may be—gospel, history, epistle, apocalypse—and whoever the writer—Luke, Paul, John, the writer to the Hebrews—the *kerygma* can be traced in the work." [10] The primitive preaching proclaimed Jesus as "Lord and Messiah"; it is his Person, his words and his work, enshrined in the kerygma, which unify the whole body of New Testament literature.

This statement, however, may appear to be contradicted by the first contribution to Christian sacred writings—the letters of Paul. To answer such an objection, one can of course pick out here and there in Paul fragments of lapidary formulae which have a kerygmatic ring (1 Cor. 15, 3ff.; Rom. 1, 1-4; 8, 31ff.; 10, 8-9).[11] The more fundamental reply rests upon the fact that the continuing authenticity of the Christian message does not derive primarily from the apostolic memory of what Jesus said and did, but upon the Spirit-filled understanding of himself and his redemptive work. That Paul was cognizant of Jesus' teaching in parables and his sayings I have tried to show elsewhere;[12] but his awareness that his authority as a preacher of the Gospel rests upon his possession of "the mind of Christ" (1 Cor. 2, 16) gives him the assurance that if, in his letters, he adds to our Lord's teaching, he can order them read at public worship "in the Lord's name" (cf. 1 Thess. 5, 27; Col. 4, 16), since this living tradition is simply an expansion of the kerygma. The superstructure which Paul builds rests upon "Jesus Christ himself" (1 Cor. 3, 10ff.).

The Apocalypse is simply the kerygma transposed into an apocalyptic key. Its central message that the risen Christ is Lord

[10] A. Hunter, *op. cit.*, p. 70.

[11] C. H. Dodd, *History and the Gospel* (London, ²1964): "The Historical Tradition in the New Testament," pp. 29-52.

[12] D. Stanley, "Pauline Allusions to the Sayings of Jesus," in *Cath. Bibl. Quart.* 23 (1961), pp. 26-39.

of history is the major theme of the apostolic preaching. The written gospels, the supreme theological literary achievement of the apostolic Church, in their turn are actually the fourfold orchestration of the kerygma. What is perhaps not so fully appreciated, however, is that they really represent four very personal "spiritualities" whose creation depends (like that of the Pauline letters) more upon the creative dynamism of the Spirit than upon any mere reminiscence, however accurate, of the "brute facts" concerning Jesus' earthly career. Their essential quality as "Good News" springs from this living witness of Christian faith by four privileged representatives of the apostolic Church, which indeed truly incarnates the *dicta et facta Jesu,* but yet words and deeds which were selected, interpreted and sometimes transposed so as to serve the divine purpose of presenting the *saving truth* of "the Word of this salvation" (Acts 13, 26).

Jules Cambier, S.D.B. / *Leopoldville, Rep. of the Congo*

Paul and Tradition

I n Paul's thought Christian tradition is *the explanation of the event of Christ,* faithfully given and lived in the Churches; all that has been revealed by God before Christ must be seen anew through Christ and become Christian teaching and tradition. The apostles are the stewards of the mysteries of God (1 Cor. 4, 1) and servants of the divine action which operates in the Church and molds Christians in faithfulness to Christ. This is primarily faithfulness to the words of the Lord and to the Gospel revealed to Paul, but Paul also possesses a faithfulness to the Spirit of the Lord to explain the event of Christ and so conform his hearers to the life of Christ.

Tradition thus becomes the expression of the living faithfulness of the Church to the person and the Gospel of Christ, foretold and described in the scriptures and now revealed in the event of Christ. It is enriched through Paul's charismatic meditations and transmitted by him to his communities *to form them in the Christian life.* Finally, according to Paul, this tradition has its own characteristically *Christian style*—that of *freedom,* the mark that distinguishes true Christian vocation and life. This is an intense and living faithfulness to the words of the Lord and to the traditions that refer directly to his person; it is also a faithfulness to the spirit of a number of traditions that are bound up with a particular cultural background, but whose external form can change through respect for the same faithfulness to the Spirit who animates them. The spirit of the Pauline tradition can be summed up as follows: faithfulness to Christ, life in Christ and Christian freedom.[1]

I

CHRIST, THE ORIGIN AND INSPIRATION OF THE PAULINE TRADITION

According to Paul's gospel, Christ has set us free from all the forces of evil (sin and death), from the domination of all heavenly powers which now are subject to him (Eph. 1, 21), as well as from every compulsion of human origin: from the rule of the Law (Gal. 5, 1) and from all the powers of the earth (Gal. 4, 3). This Christian freedom enables us to express our submission and our obedience to God through the mediation of our Lord Jesus Christ. A religion demanding such sincere recognition of the person and the power of God could not arise spontaneously; if this had happened we would undoubtedly have an expression of what is best in man commingled with the baser elements as well, but not a true response to and acceptance of God, a complete and genuine submission of the whole of our person to God.

Acceptance of the Gospel of Christ in faith and obedience to God is expressed in a form of religious life whose foundation is the spiritual understanding of the event of Christ (1 Cor. 15), the words and the example of Christ (cf. 2 Cor. 10, 1), as well as the privileged and authoritative interpretations of these as given by the charismatic "spirituals", principally "the apostles and prophets" (cf. Eph. 2, 20; 3, 5), the founders of the communities, among whom Paul places himself first. The ministry of the apostle resulted in doctrinal traditions that were an expression of faith in Christ and in traditions of Christian behavior that expressed the faith as lived out in practice according to the cultural background of the day. The first of these traditions are

[1] A good bibliography on the subject will be found in B. Gerhardsson, *Memory and Manuscript* (Lund, [2]1964).

privileged and of absolute authority; the second are to be accepted insofar as they permit witness to the truth and to the charity of Christ.

In fact, not all the teaching about the person and the life of Christ as an example for Christians was written down, and Paul himself never told us in writing all that he knew and understood about Christ. But the whole of Christian life must start from the Gospel of Christ and be an expression of him. To describe the gospel revelation that he had received, Paul used an expression signifying a tradition that has been faithfully received: "I *received* the gospel . . . through a revelation of Jesus Christ" (Gal. 1, 12). We read the word "receive" (*paralambanein*) again in the well-known passages of 1 Corinthians 11, 23 and 15, 3 where it forms one part of the technical doublet "to receive—to transmit" (*paralambanein-paradidonai*): the Christian teaching is received and then transmitted in faithfulness to Christ. He even describes his vocation as an apostle with an eye to its associations with the notion of tradition, although he broadened this a little; even if he had never lived with the Lord from the time of the baptism of John the Baptist to the day of his glorification and so become a witness to his resurrection (cf. Acts 1, 22), at least he had seen the risen Christ (Gal. 1, 16; 1 Cor. 9, 1; 15, 8) and of this he was a witness (1 Cor. 1, 6), an apostle (cf. the beginnings of all his letters) and servant (1 Cor. 4, 1; 2 Cor. 10, 1ff.; Eph. 3, 7). Therefore, like the other apostles, Paul is an authorized witness to the Christian message and a founder of the Christian doctrinal tradition; he is a true witness to Christ because he possesses his Spirit; in no way does he resemble the pseudo-apostles of Corinth who preach only themselves (2 Cor. 4, 5) and distort the message of the gospel (2 Cor. 2, 17).

Christ is the foundation and the only source of Paul's gospel, either directly through a revelation received from Christ—in the heat of controversy, as, for example, in Galatians, Paul insisted very much on this point—or indirectly through the traditions of Jerusalem: the words of the Lord he quoted and the "traditions of the Churches" he insisted that his communities adopt. Sufficient emphasis has not always been placed on the importance that Paul attributed to the criterion of the faith of Jerusalem and the witness of the Twelve in establishing Christian truth (cf. the important testimony in the otherwise polemic passage of Gal. 2, 2). For Paul as well, Jerusalem remained by the will of the Lord Jesus the place from which the Word of God went out to the world and the first center from which its luster spread abroad. Luke hardly exaggerates Paul's position when, in the *program-logion* of Acts, he writes: "And you shall be my witnesses in Jerusalem and in all Judea and Samaria and to the ends of the earth" (Acts 1, 8b); he carefully notes every occasion that Paul returns to Jerusalem and it is probable that he even adds to their number (cf. in particular Acts 2, 27-30).[2]

But we must also remember the way in which Paul saw the whole field of his apostolic endeavor (Rom. 15, 19), his advice to imitate the Church of Jerusalem (1 Thess. 2, 14), the collection that he organized for the poor of Jerusalem and which lay so close to his heart during the final year of his apostolic ministry. He took the traditions of the Churches of Judea and imposed them on the Greek Churches (1 Cor. 2, 2-16). And if to strengthen his authority as an apostle he proves that through the will of Christ his position is on the same level as that of Peter's, this is not to set himself up against Peter; his assertion is rather an indirect testimony to the authority of Peter and of the Church of Jerusalem (Gal. 2, 7).

Thus "the tradition", either received directly from Christ or indirectly through the communities of Judea, is normative for the life of the Pauline communities. Paul transmits these traditions and imposes them, every now and then indirectly recalling the privileged position of Jerusalem (1 Cor. 14, 36). The ultimate explanation of this is that the same Christ, who was revealed to Paul and who was also the object of the Palestinian tradition, was the source of the tradition forming the faithful in the Christian life.

[2] Cf. J. C. Cambier, "Le voyage de S. Paul à Jerusalem en Act. IX, 26ss. et le schéma missionaire théologique de S. Luc," in *N. T. Stud.* 8 (1961/62), pp. 249-57.

II

TRADITION SHAPED THE CHRISTIAN LIFE IN THE PAULINE COMMUNITIES

Paul received from Christ the authority he needed to build up his communities (2 Cor. 10, 8), but he could do this only according to the truth (2 Cor. 13, 8) and on the foundation which is Christ (1 Cor. 3, 1ff.; the same idea is expressed through another image in Ephesians 2, 20-22). Paul can allow no other Gospel than the one he preaches (Gal. 1, 6-9), and this can be summed up as Christ crucified (1 Cor. 1, 18. 23; 2, 2); to this central point he relates all that he has to say about Christ.

In the first place we must mention the two privileged traditions of Christ's resurrection and the Last Supper; it is quite characteristic of Paul's approach that he reminds the community of Corinth about them, for its libertarian spirit was not an expression of Christian freedom but rather of a sense of its own importance. With decided irony Paul reminds them that the gospel tradition did not originate with them (1 Cor. 14, 36), and he does this when recalling a Jewish custom, adopted by the Christian communities of Palestine, which he orders them to observe (14, 34): "As in all the Churches of the saints, the women should keep silent in the Churches." In his recounting of the two privileged traditions, we can see at once how the gospel message and tradition are intertwined, the tradition being the expression of the gospel message. Just as he "received" his gospel from Christ and from God himself (Gal. 1, 12. 16), so he also "received" the testimony of the resurrection of Christ: the Corinthians received it from Paul who transmitted to them the message that he himself had "received". This important message of 1 Corinthians 15, 1-11 brings this out well; in the same way as a rabbinical tradition is proposed by citing the links in the chain of its transmission, so Paul sets down in detail the list of witnesses, closing this list with the name of Paul himself who is quoting the tradition. As the Jews also did, Paul links up tradition with scripture.

The same thing takes place in the other privileged tradition concerning the Last Supper of the Lord (1 Cor. 11, 23-27).

The Corinthians who did not celebrate the eucharist in true
Christian fashion have not preserved the tradition that Paul transmitted to them and which he himself had "received" as coming
from the Lord. Here we have a reference to a tradition going
back to one of the Lord's actions, just as on other occasions he
refers to a tradition reporting the Lord's words: e.g., the indis-
solubility of marriage (1 Cor. 7, 10ff.; cf. Mk. 10, 11ff. and
parallels), or, again, the Lord's saying that the laborer is worthy
of his wages (1 Cor. 9, 14; cf. Mt. 10, 10 and Lk. 10, 7).

Another way in which Paul associates himself with the tradition of the Lord Jesus is in his charismatic interpretation of the
reality of the Christian faith when he is induced to propose a
particular line of conduct to his believers. All the time he makes
it clear that here he is not ascribing this to the Lord's words but
to his own charismatic understanding of the Christian life; this
is the case when he advises that celibacy should be preserved
(1 Cor. 7, 15ff.). There are other traditions that Paul imposes
on all his Churches, such as remaining in the same social con-
dition as at the time of being called to the Christian life; thus a
slave should not demand his freedom just because he has become
a Christian (1 Cor. 7, 17). It is very possible that this last injunction was a practical measure directed against the only too
human and selfish ambitions of those in slavery to whom Paul
wanted to bring home that the essential thing in life is belonging
to Christ (7, 22). Still other traditions are customs that Paul as a
good Jew naturally took over from the Churches of Palestine
(cf. 1 Cor. 2, 16), such as the obligation of women to cover their
heads when they were present at the meetings of the Christian
community (1 Cor. 11, 3ff.), and also keeping silent in these
gatherings (1 Cor. 14, 34). These practical rules are part of the
Christian traditions that Paul orders his communities to preserve
(1 Cor. 11, 2). I think that here you could also add the way in
which Paul suggests that married people should live their lives
together on the basis of a domination-subjection relationship,
the husband ruling his wife and she obeying her husband in all
things. What he is recommending to married couples is essentially

Christian love, lived out and expressed from day to day in the established order of his time.

The permanent core of Paul's practical directive is the Christian love that should inspire conjugal life. The forms that human social life takes can vary with the country and with the evolution of culture. Because they are inspired by truth and charity, there can be quite another different but still Christian way of leading the married life on the basis of mutual dialogue.[3]

From this example we can see quite clearly how the Christian tradition must be preserved in its essential spirit, while at the same time being expressed in different ways according to different cultural and historical situations. The essential and permanent factor is devotion to the person and teaching of the Lord Jesus. Therefore, tradition is not something standing apart from scripture, but rather an explanation of scripture, drawing its whole validity from it. It is not a second source of Christian teaching, but an explanation and development of the one unique source: namely, the words and actions of Christ that illustrate and enrich the basic Christian event of the death and resurrection of Christ, the privileged and unchanging foundation of the Christian tradition. All this taken together formed the Pauline Christian communities.

Bearing in mind this purpose of building up his communities, we must examine two of the ways in which this tradition was enriched. One way in which tradition was developed was bound up with a technical method used in Jewish rabbinical teaching. From the beginning it was adopted by the first Palestinian community and no doubt by Jesus himself before this. It consisted in reading the scriptures and finding Christian teaching in them. Like the rabbis, Paul made use of this technique to explain his gospel through the texts of scripture and to justify the traditions that he recommended to his communities. The method used most frequently by the rabbis was to choose a text containing a key word which was expressly found in the formulation of the tradition

[3] Cf. *idem*, "Le grand mystère concernant le Christ et son Englise en Eph. 5, 22-33," in *Biblica* 47 (1966), pp. 43-90, 223-42.

they wished to defend and explain; they then went on to interpret the text they had chosen in the sense of the tradition they were proposing. For the Jews the "cipher" used in commenting on scripture was the Jewish tradition of a particular school or that proposed by some respected rabbi; then a list of authorities was cited and this reinforced the solidity of the tradition. For Paul, the "cipher" giving the key to the understanding of the scriptural text he was using was the person of Christ, and this was how he hoped to foster Christian customs and behavior among his faithful people. Thus Genesis 1, 27—"man, the image of God"—with his added commentary—"and the glory of God"—should convince women to wear a veil in the Christian assemblies. And Isaiah 28, 11ff. with a short scriptural pastiche tagged on (1 Cor. 14, 25) ought to be enough to persuade the Corinthians to speak more in "prophecy" and less in "tongues", thus helping to build up the community in Christ. A catena of scriptural texts should be sufficient to prevent the Corinthians ranging themselves alongside the pseudo-apostles who scorned the apostle who had established the community.

Paul was within his rights to read scripture in this way because he was a charismatic. It was also as an apostle of the gospel and as a charismatic that he molded his communities in the traditions of the Christian life. Paul's personality and talents are the means through which the gift of God is transmitted: a gift merited by Christ and to be followed according to God's will.

As far back as his very first letter to the Thessalonians, he speaks of his apostolate as a transmission of the Christian tradition which enables believers to live in a Christian fashion to please God. (2, 14; 4, 1). In the second letter to them a little time afterward he reminds them again of this (2 Thess. 2, 15). In one of his last letters a characteristic passage shows him as the preacher of the Gospel and as one shaping his communities in the Christian tradition he had implanted among the Gentile Churches. After having confirmed that everything inspired by justice and holiness could have a place in Christian morality (Phil. 4, 8), he goes on: What you have learned (through the

Christian catechesis), what you have "received" (as being Christian tradition), what you know of my own person through having heard and seen me (the theme of the imitation of the apostle), all this do you also (4, 9).

To ensure the formation of his faithful in Christ Paul places great reliance on the charismatics of the Churches, among whom must be numbered the presidents of the communities, for their actions are the manifestation of God's action in the communities, and especially that of the Holy Spirit (cf. 1 Cor. 12, 4-11). Each of them must use his particular gifts in charity for the purpose of building up the community, not allowing personal ambitions to intervene, inasmuch as they have nothing to do with the gift of faith that continually must be lived up to through the exercise of the various charismatic gifts (cf. Rom. 12, 3-8). The same advice underlies the whole of the passage of 1 Corinthians 12—14: the purpose of the exercise of charismatic gifts is the building up and the formation of the faithful. From the time when he wrote the letters to the Corinthians, Paul emphasizes the charisms of knowledge, and this appears again even more in Ephesians 4, 1-16: the Church is built up as the faithful acquires a more perfect knowledge of Christ, and this is brought about through the work of those possessing the gifts of knowledge, which in this context must mean the charismatics as the leaders of the communities: apostles, prophets, evangelists, pastors and teachers (4, 13).

This brings out very clearly that for Paul the heads of the communities are first of all educators in the faith. This explains the importance he attaches to the preaching of the message in the establishment and the formation of the Churches, as also the important role of the apostle and prophet in the Pauline communities. They are the servants of the message and their function is to exhort the faithful and to build them up in Christ. They continue the ministry of the ancient prophets in Israel; the Church that they establish and build up is in fact the continuation of the Church and the assembly of the desert, but this time it possesses the fullness of the revelation of the love of God.

Observing tradition and the traditions of the Churches helps the Church to be maintained in the unity desired by its founder, the Lord Jesus. If in proposing Christian tradition a man allows it to be colored with his own personal viewpoint so that his own ambitions and personal talents are given pride of place, such a man is a traitor to Christ. Sometimes to avoid divisions in the communities Paul is obliged to reassert his authority as an apostle in rigorous fashion (cf. especially 2 Cor. 10, 8-13) and to build up and unite the communities; in the same way he demands that the faithful recognize the authority of the presidents of the communities and also love them (1 Thess. 5, 12ff.; we find the same injunction in 1 Cor. 16, 3; Rom. 16, 23; Col. 4, 15).

With the same purpose in view, Paul also reminds his readers of the authority possessed by the brethren delegated by him to lead a community or to root out abuses that had crept in; he urged this in the case of Timothy (1 Cor. 4, 17) and Titus (2 Cor. 12, 18) whom he sent to the Church of the Corinthians. So it was that toward the end of Paul's life, with the development of the Church, traditions of Church government came into being (cf. Phil. 1, 1; cf. also 1 Tim. 3, 2. 8. 12; Tit. 1, 7). Despite what some critics have said in connection with Galatians 1, 18 and 2, 2, Paul recognized Peter's position in the Church just as it appears in early tradition and in the gospels as well.[4]

In his practical task of forming the lives of his communities, Paul always gave prominence to his own exceptional role, not through any need he felt to dominate, but because of the commission he had received from Christ to build up the one single Church. Paul knew that he was responsible for the preaching of the Gospel to the nations (Gal. 2, 7-9), and his whole life was consecrated to this task. He strove to reproduce the image of Christ in himself, to put on Christ, to the point of being able to say that it was no longer he but Christ who lived within him. He could also say to his faithful: You have become my imitators, just as you have become the imitators of Christ (1 Thess. 1, 6), and as you have become the imitators of "the Christian Churches

---

[4] For the formation of Christian traditions in the development of the Churches established by St. Paul, cf. *idem*, "Paul," in *Dict. Bibl. Suppl.*, coll. 325-29, 368-73.

which are in Judea" (1 Thess. 2, 14). He recommends that the Philippians take him as their example so as not to range themselves among the enemies of Christ (Phil. 3, 17ff.).

Paul proposes his own life, a life lived by faith, as an example to be followed by his Christian people. He does this in a particularly striking fashion when writing to the Corinthians whom he desires to form in the basic Christian virtue of humility (cf. 2 Cor. 10, 1). In the same line of thought and to help the Corinthians he describes his apostolic life as being an expression of his life of faith, a life that is also one of humility. That the glory of God may be seen more clearly he acquiesces in living out his ministry in weakness and dishonor; in this way the fruit of his apostolate is clearly shown to be entirely due to the intervention of the power of God alone. The example of his life and of his apostolate was for the Christians of his day, and for those of the future, a tradition of the Christian life and an expression of faith and faithfulness to Christ.[5]

Paul's primary concern as he formed his communities was to inspire in them the faith and the Christian freedom which manifests itself in charity. Furthermore, the order that Paul commands to be observed in the assemblies for worship is not some ideal standard of order established once and for all, but a way of regulating the conduct of the assembly so as to provide further edification, that is, a better knowledge of the gospel and of the revelation of God, thus ensuring that a more perfect praise and thanksgiving is rendered to God. This whole practical formation given by the apostles and the charismatics is the expression of the life of Christ and of the Spirit living in the Church. The scriptures, the revelation of the event of Christ and also the examples and the words of the Lord Jesus are its foundation. The directives of Paul and of the charismatics and presidents of the communities are its explanation and practical application—indeed, the beginnings of a living tradition not standing apart from scripture, but proceeding from the Word of God and from Christ.

[5] *Idem*, "Le critère paulinien de l'apostolat en 2 Cor. 12, 6ff.," in *Biblica* 43 (1963), pp. 481-518.

This living tradition has continued in the Church according to the needs of the Christian life, being adapted to the various situations in which the Church has been implanted. No doubt there has not always been a sufficiently clear distinction drawn between the great tradition which is directly conceived with the Word of God and the event of Christ on the one hand, and, on the other, the contingent forms of its expression that are conditioned by the particular cultural environment. The danger of an ossification of tradition can be avoided if we always first remember the real essence of the Pauline tradition—namely, an expression of our faithfulness to Christ—and also if we ensure that tradition always contains its twofold Pauline characteristic: i.e., Christian freedom and life. In practice these two points of view are fused together: Christian freedom is the actual concrete way in which Christians express their faithfulness to Christ according to the customs of their own day. This presupposes Christian submissiveness toward ecclesial authority. Submissiveness and freedom, to the extent that they are truly Christian, are complementary values. Traditions for Paul are not a human institution, but a human expression of the truth of Christ lived in charity.

III

THE SPIRIT OF THE PAULINE TRADITION

The Pauline tradition that molded his communities sought to develop that true Christian freedom which expresses itself in consecration to God and in fraternal charity. This "Christian order" that Paul wished to see as the inspiring force within his communities has nothing static or rigid about it. The "spirituals", with Paul foremost among them, are those who educate the faithful and who at the same time are the moving spirits and guides of a living tradition. This tradition is marked by a freedom and a life that spontaneously flowers into true faithfulness to the Lord Jesus. It is because the "spirituals" are led by the Spirit and because the life of Christ dwells within their hearts (Eph. 3, 16ff.) that they are called to exercise their ministry for the purpose of building up the Church (Eph. 4, 11-16). This dynamic order, strengthened by the traditions imposed by Paul, is the fruit of a living faith through which the Spirit of God himself, the source of freedom and quickening of life, continually operates. When Paul wants to justify his authority to impose rules of conduct, he backs up his actions by pointing to the fact that he has been approved by the Lord (1 Cor. 7, 25) and that he possesses the Spirit of God (7, 40).

The Spirit who stirred up Paul's heart and the hearts of the charismatics of his day continues his action throughout the whole span of the history of the Church, so long as he is not deprived of his freedom of action (cf. 1 Thess. 5, 19); it is he who breathes life into Christian order and makes it throb with life. Thus to remain true and "spiritual", Christian tradition can and sometimes must alter the form in which it is expressed. Tradition can never justify a lack of reflection and self-renewal. Christians, who by definition are people consecrated to God and who love and serve their brethren, quite naturally change some of the outward forms of their worship and, most of all, the types of service they render to their fellowman. They cannot just put off changing one particular form of Christian witness, which is now outdated and incomprehensible to their contemporaries, until their way of life has cut them off from the world in which they have the obligation of confessing Christ so as to make him known and accepted by all men. Because of this, Paul was opposed to traditions and ways of life which, because of particular circumstances, threatened to be prejudicial to the truth of the Gospel (Gal. 2, 14). Everything that ecclesial authority proposes or imposes must be determined by bearing in mind the truth of Christ and for the purpose of building up the Church (2 Cor. 13, 8). These Pauline criteria of truth are to be applied to the evolution of traditions, for they are the expressions of Christ which vary with the particular time and culture. One can, for example, be faithful to the true Christian tradition without forcing all women, independently of local custom, to cover their heads in our churches (cf. *supra,* p. 106). What fostered Christian discipline and order in the context of the customs of a past age, even that of the early Church, can perhaps be no longer useful in preserving a spirit of faithfulness to Christ; this spirit is the only thing that matters and it is tradition's mission to preserve it in the Christian Church. For this reason, tradition is a spirit of freedom at the same time that it is a spirit of faithfulness. By definition it involves the possibility of evolution, inasmuch as its role is to foster the living faithfulness of Christians to the Lord so that this might be a witness to the gospel in the particular surroundings in which they live.

Christian tradition, as the expression of this living faithfulness to the Lord Jesus, has nothing of the rigidity of the "traditions of the fathers" of which Paul himself has been a zealous observer before he came to count them all as refuse from the time that he came to know Christ Jesus (Phil. 3, 4-8). The "traditions of the fathers" demanded stability in the forms of Jewish religious life: the living power of the Christian traditions stems from Christ and from his Spirit. For it is Christ and his Spirit who form and direct the Church to the precise extent that the Church is faithful to the freedom of the Spirit and to the life in Christ.

IV

CONCLUSION

The spiritual understanding of Christ is the soul of the living tradition of Christianity, just as the Lord Jesus is the center of the gospel and of every aspect of Christian life. Tradition includes teachings to be believed and also ways of life that are the authorized expression of these beliefs. We find Paul narrating traditions about the resurrection of Christ or the celebration of the Last Supper, traditional formulas recalling Christ's death whose purpose was to obtain for us the justification of God (cf. Rom. 4, 23-25). Besides these he also set forward ways of living the Christian life (e.g., celibacy: 1 Cor. 7, 25-40), or of taking part in meetings for worship, or, again, practical decisions for the government of his Churches: all this is the fruit of the apostle's spiritual understanding of the event of Christ.

The essential basis of Christian faith and life is the event of the Lord Jesus, the words of God in the bible and also the words and commandments of the Lord Jesus. The instruction and directives of the charismatics, and first of all of Paul himself, also help to shape Christian life and faith because they possess the Spirit of the Lord. In the religious organization of the Christian faith they are the means through which the power of God passes, justifying and transforming his faithful. According to Paul, one cannot distinguish two different sources of the divine revelation and action among men. All comes from the Word of God understood in the light of the event of Christ and of the words and example of the life of Christ Jesus. The developments brought about by Paul and the charismatics, directing and shaping the communities, are the fruit of the Christian life and of the spiritual understanding of the divine revelation; they cannot be looked upon merely as something introduced or added on or of completely different natures. They draw all their power and value from the Word of God revealed in the religious organization of the Christian life, from which they can be distinguished but never separated.

Tradition is the expression of the Christian faith and life, nourished by the Word of God, which expresses this Word in the life of the Church. Paul, the preacher of the gospel of freedom, is also the defender of a living tradition. It is tradition that enables freedom to be Christian: that is, to be a freedom that leads to the consecration of our lives to God and the building up and strengthening of our brethren.

PART II
BIBLIOGRAPHICAL
SURVEY

Thierry Maertens / *Bruges, Belgium*

French Literature on the Homily

In undertaking to write this bibliographical summary at the request of the editor of *Concilium*, I find myself in the position both of judge and interested party, for I have already considered it my duty to take part in the discussions concerning the definition of the homily and in the work of preparing the necessary instruments for placing the homily in its proper setting. I hope that the views and attitudes I have formed will not impair the objectivity of these notes.

I will not go back any further than 1963, since Vatican Council II made quite an outstanding restatement of the principles of homiletics (cf. *Constitution on the Sacred Liturgy*, nn. 35, 52).

Definition of the Homily

The best collection of articles on this subject is that contained in *Maison-Dieu* 82 (1965). The article by Joseph Gelineau ("L'homélie, forme plénière de la prédication": pp. 29-42) rightly raises the problem of its literary genre: as an integral part of the liturgical celebration the homily is neither evangelization nor apologetics; it is not even catechesis proper.[1] It is an element

---

[1] It does not seem likely, therefore, that studies of the homily and plans of homilies conceived with the intention of linking catechesis and homily have any chance of serving the future requirements of homiletics proper. Such is the case, in particular, with the work of Elie Fournier, "Quand le Concile parle de l'homélie," in *Lumen Vitae* (1963), pp. 739-55, and the

in that moment of the history of salvation made up by the liturgi-cal celebration. The very efficacity of the homily stems from the eucharistic Word, for which it acts as a preparation, and also from the Word proclaimed in those readings on which it is based.[2] It could be said, therefore, that, while being a commentary upon the biblical readings proclaimed, the homily reveals through them the extent of the history of salvation contained in the liturgi-cal celebration itself [3] and the significance for salvation of the conduct of Christians living their daily lives.

This definition expressed by Vatican Council II has been the inspiration for the principal articles on the homily. It links the homily first with the sacred text upon which it comments, and secondly with life, which it renders "significant". There are well-known difficulties experienced by some Protestant ministers who have been too much influenced by a certain negative exegesis to make a valid commentary on a biblical text. However, Claude Wiener in an article entitled "Exégèse et annonce de la Parole" [4] admirably sets forth several guiding principles that enable a minister to take into account the strictest exegesis while adopting a position within the bounds of learned hypothesis and research. There is no doubt on this score that ministers will be able in-creasingly to profit by exegetical science and proclaim the Word of God in all its authenticity.

However, the history of salvation is not only described in the

---

same author's *Prédication pastorale et renouveau liturgique: I. Le Credo; II. Les sacrements; III. Les commandements* (Brussels: Ed. Lumen Vitae, 1963-1965).

[2] Worthy of notice is A. M. Roguet's doctrinal study, "La présence active du Christ dans la Parole de Dieu," in the same issue of *Maison-Dieu* 82 (1965), pp. 8-28. Also worth noting are M. Didier's more concise "L'homélie. Doctrine et suggestions concrètes," in *Rev. Dioc. Namur* (1964), pp. 248-67, and G. Bernard's "L'homélie," *ibid.* (1965), pp. 310-31.

[3] That is, the commentary on the Mass tends to become "mystagogy" and to extend the efficacy of the homily itself over the entire celebration. I have deemed it advisable to insist upon this union of homily and com-mentary in the introduction to *Schémas de monitions liturgiques pour chaque dimanche* (Ed. Biblica, 1966).

[4] In the same issue of *Maison-Dieu*, n. 82, pp. 59-76.

scriptures; events, ways of thinking and the boundaries of modern thought also make up the elements of a history in which God speaks to man and where the minister, precisely by means of his homily, must be integrated into the celebration. In my opinion[5] the celebrant is not merely a person who declares what is contained in the biblical readings proclaimed, but also one who becomes, as it were, a mediator between Word of God in the bible and Word of God in life. Moreover, the problem is not a simple one, and it is safe to predict that sometime in the near future we shall see the publication of a survey on the homily, in which the works analyzed will be especially concerned with the integration of biblical and modern cultures.

The Material

First of all, let us state the boundaries of the investigation. The general commentaries on the liturgical year will not be examined here, nor will the books for the commentator or such essential tools as dictionaries of biblical themes, missals, etc. Only works concerned directly with the preparation of the homily will be considered.

It is interesting to note that Canada set aside a study session to discuss "the liturgical years and preaching" (Montreal: January, 1965). Unfortunately, the only information we have about it is in a brief review.[6] However, a richer source of information is to be found in the majority of magazines devoted to biblical and liturgical ministry. *Notes de pastorale liturgique* from n. 51 (July, 1964) onward have supplied a very well written commentary on the gospels and epistles.[7] The author gives a general summary of text and context and goes on to make a literal commentary, pointing out the difficult and most important words and then pausing to reveal their profundity. The reader thus easily

[5] Thierry Maertens, "La messe demain: une vraie célébration dans la vie des gens," in *Par. Lit.* (1965), pp. 511-26.

[6] J. Beaulac, "Dixième session d'etudes sur la prédication," in *Communauté Chrétienne* (1965), pp. 102-04.

[7] A. M. Roguet, *Commentaire littéral des évangiles des dimanches* (nn. 51-56); *Commentaire littéral des épîtres du dimanche* (nn. 55ff.).

grasps the meaning of the text, but at this point he is left to his own resources by the author and is free to select the theme of his homily. Quite a similar method as regards both the epistle and the gospel is to be found in *Bible et vie chrétienne,* in which "Matériaux pour l'homélie dominicale" [8] by Hilaire Duesberg has been appearing since n. 61 (early 1965).

The characteristic feature of these two series is the exclusive recourse they have to exegesis. They are absolutely "non-directive", hardly taking into account the liturgical context of the celebration or the social conditions or status of the congregation. It will not be surprising, therefore, to find other accounts which attempt to go further and provide an analysis of the liturgical formulary, doctrinal study and pastoral application, as well as the necessary exegetical information.

There are two large collections of material to be considered now in this connection. The first, *Assemblées du Seigneur,*[9] can be regarded as a veritable encyclopedia of the liturgical year, and here the exegetical and liturgical analyses particularly stand out. The dominant principle in this collection is also non-directive. Nevertheless, the theological and pastoral commentaries select a theme from the formulary and, in connection with this theme, present valid analyses. Sometimes, however, these are adventitious and do not necessarily lead to an understanding of the celebration proper.

The other collection comprises only five volumes of 250 pages each. *Guide for the Christian Assembly,*[10] edited by Thierry

[8] Mention must also be made of many other magazines: *Feu Nouveau,* containing an article entitled "Célébrons l'Eucharistie", which also supplies material outside the scope of the problem of the homily; *Communauté Chrétienne,* containing "Pour l'homélie de chaque dimanche" by L. A. Gignac; *Parole et Pain,* containing "La Parole dans l'assemblée"; lastly, *Paroisse et Liturgie,* containing "Homélie et commentaire pour chaque dimanche de l'année".

[9] Editions Biblica (Bruges-Paris). A hundred-page volume for every Sunday; 55 volumes were published between 1962 and 1966. Spanish translation: *Asambleas del Señor* (Ed. Marova, Madrid); 38 volumes were published between 1964 and 1966.

[10] Ed. Casterman, Paris-Tournai (1964-66). Dutch translation, in collaboration with Godfried Danneels and Anton Nuij: *Gids voor de liturgi-*

Maertens and Jean Frisque, provides exegetical commentary
(usually non-original), readings, liturgical analysis and doctrinal
study. The characteristic feature of this work is that is it more
directive than the preceding ones. The exegetical study in it
tends to determine one or two important themes, and the analysis
of the composition of the liturgical formulary also has a similar
tendency. In liturgical circles this is, admittedly, the most debated
point about this method.

However, the authors believe that they have some justification;
they hold the view that the homily must act as a link between the
bible, life and the celebration. This requirement eliminates many
themes that would otherwise be possible. Nevertheless, it would
be to their interest, in any future printing of the book, occasionally to suggest a supplementary theme so as to avoid being taxed
with systematism. The selected doctrinal analysis for every Sunday is, however, by no means adventitious: it succeeds in embracing in one synthetic vision the history of salvation, the person
of Christ and the history of the Church, together with a view of
the contemporary world. There can be no doubt that such an all-
embracing synthesis makes the celebration comprehensible, insofar as the minister is able to incorporate it into his homily.

---

sche gemeenschapsviering (Ed. Biblica, Bruges), 3 vols. published. English
translation: *Guide for the Christian Assembly* (Ed. Biblica, Bruges), 5
vols. published. German translation: *Kommentar zum Messbuch* (Ed.
Herder, Freiburg), 5 vols. published. Spanish translation: *Guia de la
asamblea cristiana* (Ed. Marova, Madrid, and D.D.B., Bilbao), 4 vols.
published. Italian translation, *Guida il messale della assemblea* (Ed. Elle
Di Ci, Turin), 5 vols. published. Portuguese translation in preparation.
Furthermore, these works have led to the publication, in these various
languages, of several missals based on the *Missel de l'assemblée chretienne*.
In addition, these volumes have been adapted for the catechesis of
children, under the title of *Initiation des enfants à la liturgie dominicale*,
5 vols. (Ed. Biblica, Bruges-Paris).

Gerard S. Sloyan/*Washington, D.C.*

English Literature on the Homily

While literature on preaching in English is fairly copious, treatment of the homily as part of the liturgy is far less abundant.[1] The reasons should be obvious to all. The Roman Catholic community—theologians, preachers and people alike—has tended to put a relatively low value on the

[1] Some of the Catholic writing available in translation which is proving helpful in the preparation of homilies would include: W. Bulst, *Revelation* (New York: Herder and Herder, 1964); D. Grasso, *Proclaiming God's Message* (Notre Dame, Ind.: University of Notre Dame, 1965), undoubtedly the best single treatment of the theology of preaching; P. Hitz, *To Preach The Gospel* (New York: Sheed and Ward, 1963); T. Maertens, *Bible Themes*, 2 vols. (Bruges: DDB, 1965); T. Maertens and J. Frisque, *Guide for the Christian Assembly*, 5 vols. (Bruges: Biblica, 1965), a rich source book which provides "exegesis, liturgical analysis, a biblical theme, and doctrine" in conjunction with each of the Sundays and major feasts; G. Michonneau and F. Varillon, *From Pulpit to People* (Westminster, Md.: Newman Press, 1965); A. G. Martimort *et al.*, *The Liturgy and the Word of God* (Collegeville, Minn.: Liturgical Press, 1959); O. Semmelroth, *The Preaching Word* (New York: Sheed and Ward, 1965); H. Urs von Balthasar, *Word and Revelation*. Essays in Theology, 2 vols. (New York: Herder and Herder, 1964); *idem, Word and Redemption* (New York: Herder and Herder, 1965).

Some Protestant titles of value include: J.-J. von Allmen, *Preaching and Congregation* (London: SCM; Richmond, Va.: John Knox, 1962); K. Barth, *The Preaching of the Gospel* (Philadelphia: Westminster, 1963); W. Hahn, *Worship and Congregation* (London: Lutterworth, 1963); D. Ritschl, *A Theology of Proclamation* (Richmond, Va.: John Knox, 1960); G. Wingren, *The Living Word* (London: SCM, 1960); *idem, Gospel and Church* (Edinburgh: Oliver and Boyd, 1964).

proclaimed Word in its insistence on sacramental efficacy. At the same time, only a halting progress has been made in understanding the true working of the sacraments; otherwise a theology of the Word would have been developed concurrently. With the rediscovery of the sacraments as signs of faith and worshipful celebrations of God's Word, an awareness of the importance of verbal proclamation as part of the "full sign" of Christ has begun to develop.

All this is to say that the fate of the homily in English-speaking countries has paralleled that of the liturgy, which in turn has depended directly on progress in the theology of Word and sacrament. Several decades of pre-theological groundwork in biblical exegesis were necessary before the inspired books could be seen in their true light: namely, as God's Word to man first delivered in a context of man's prayerful reflection on his deeds. The critical study of scripture in the Catholic Church was the pre-condition for knowing intimately its character as proclamation anticipatory of covenanted praise.

It is hard to date the beginnings of a ground swell in English-language writing, but one feels safe in naming the appearance of a slim volume by C. H. Dodd in 1936 as a major factor in understanding the homily.[2] In his concern for exegetical preaching, in which he was joined by the Reverend Sir Edwyn Hoskyns,[3] Dodd restored to the English-speaking theological community "the distinctively biblical dimensions of grace, sin and eschatology".[4] The idea of the kingdom of God returned to Christian consciousness as the apostolic proclamation of the life, death, resurrection

[2] C. H. Dodd, *The Apostolic Preaching and Its Developments* (London: Hodder and Stoughton, 1936; New York: Harper and Brothers, 1962); also cf. the same author's *The Parables of the Kingdom* (London: Hodder and Stoughton, 1935; rev. ed.: New York: Scribner's, 1961); *According to the Scriptures: The Sub-Structure of New Testament Theology* (London: J. Nisbet, 1952; New York: Scribner's, 1953).

[3] E. Hoskyns, *Cambridge Sermons* (London: S.P.C.K.; New York: Macmillan, 1938).

[4] H. Davies, *Varieties of English Preaching 1900-1960* (London: SCM Press; Englewood Cliffs, N.J.: Prentice-Hall, 1963), p. 27; this book discusses J. H. Jewett, G. Studdert Kennedy, Ronald Knox, and H. H. Farmer among others and deals with the homily only obliquely.

and ascension of Christ, which the Church makes *anamnesis* of
in a sacred meal. No longer could one misconceive the kingdom
as a "future event or utopia", much less as the "sum total of
decent cooperative human ventures to establish a more humane
society".[5] Dodd's exegesis revealed the kingdom in its New Testament sources as the rule of God actualized in every age by the
power of his judging and saving Word. It is helpful to recall that
Bultmann and Tillich, two theologians who insist on the "Christ-
event" as that historically given, unpredictable happening which
creates the community of the Church, are greatly concerned
with preaching.[6] Dodd's stress is on the beginning of God's
mighty, saving act with Christ's coming. Eschatology is "realized"
in that the work of salvation is achieved in the cross and resurrection; the last times are an event of now. "This world has become the scene of a divine drama in which the eternal issues are
laid bare. It is the hour of decision." [7] The witness given to
Christ's saving act over the ages is itself a part of the act of salvation. God's work in Christ both is, and is not, complete.

While this fruit of New Testament scholarship—basically an
analysis of the *kerygma* as found in Acts, the Pauline epistles and
the gospels—was reaching a Protestant readership, something
like it was made available in the "theology of proclamation" contrasted by J. A. Jungmann with the speculative theology of the
seminary course. Neither stream was reaching the Catholic English-speaking homilist of the 1930's, however. Such relief as the
preacher got from the wastes of his own theological formation
came with the writings of Scheeben, Mersch, Lagrange, the
Beuron and Maria Laach schools in translation and a few pio-
neers in English like Clifford, Marmion, Michel, Vonier and
Reinhold (the latter two, significantly, German-born). The journals for clerical consumption in English-speaking countries were
not particularly helpful with respect to the homily except for
Orate Fratres (Collegeville, Minnesota, 1926; title changed to

[5] *Ibid.*
[6] Cf. R. Bultmann, *This World and the Beyond* (New York: Scribner's, 1960); P. Tillich, *The New Being* (New York: Scribner's, 1955). Bult-mann's dictum is: "Preaching itself belongs to the history of redemption."
[7] C. H. Dodd, *Parables,* rev. ed., p. 159.

Worship in 1951). Many journals which had a homiletic concern did positive harm through the restricted theological outlook of those who wrote about preaching in their pages. A unique English-language book in the 1940's was Martin Hellriegel's collection of homilies which interwove the texts of each day's Mass.[8]

Of the Catholics who published sermons in English from the 1930's through the 1950's, Bede Jarrett[9] and Ronald Knox[10] were unquestionably the most literate, though neither was a homilist properly so called. Knox published a small collection of expositions of the parables in the patristic rather than the modern scientific mold.[11]

One finds only a faint echo in English-speaking Catholic homilists of the period of Reginald Fuller's demand in his important monograph on the homily that it "build up (*oikodomein*) the Church . . . [and] draw [a man] anew into the *ecclesia*. For unless the sermon leads to the liturgical action the *ecclesia* does not go on to express itself as the *ecclesia*".[12] Only biblical preaching can produce the worshiping community afresh each time, says Fuller. Neither intellectualism, nor moralism, nor emotionalism can accomplish it. In his insistence on man's need to accept in faith the event of the redemption, Fuller writes against "relevance": "Our chief concern must be not the people's needs but the Gospel in its fullness." [13]

[8] M. Hellriegel, *The True Vine and Its Branches,* Vol. 1, "The Vine" (St. Louis: Pio Decimo, 1948).

[9] B. Jarrett, *The House of Gold. Lenten Sermons* (London: Blackfriars, 1954; *Lourdes Interpreted by the Salve Regina* (Westminster, Md.: Newman Press, 1945).

[10] R. Knox, *Occasional Sermons* (London and New York: Sheed and Ward, 1960); *The Pastoral Sermons of Ronald A. Knox* (London and New York: Sheed and Ward, 1960); *University and Anglican Sermons* (London and New York: Sheed and Ward, 1963).

[11] R. Knox, *The Mystery of the Kingdom and Other Sermons* (London and New York: Sheed and Ward, 1952).

[12] R. Fuller, *What Is Liturgical Preaching?* (London: SCM, 1957), p. 11; a similar distinction is made by C. Davis, "The Theology of Preaching," in *Preaching,* ed. R. Drury (Dublin: M. H. Gill; New York: Sheed and Ward, 1962); Davis says that preaching is a ministry which serves faith while the sacraments which presuppose faith are "correlative to sanctification" (p. 12).

[13] R. Fuller, *op. cit.,* p. 17; like Barth, Fuller rules out all but the biblical Word.

The homily is of the genus *paraklesis,* a deepening of the *kerygma* and *didache* already shared through the first preaching of the Gospel and the ethical instruction given to new converts.[14] Fuller provides examples of doctrinal and ethical epistles from the lectionary, and also the three main types of gospel *pericopae:* pronouncement stories, miracle stories and parables. In "all the miracle stories in the liturgical gospels . . . the preacher must pass from the particular miracle to the ultimate miracle of the messianic redemption which it prefigures, and thence to its re-presentation by the act of God in holy communion".[15] He is helpful on the typology of the Old Testament, holding that the oldest liturgical usage which in turn derives from the New Testament is our best guide here. He also discusses the daily homily, saying that the scripture readings uncommented on are sufficient for the small group of "regulars" but that an exception should be made on greater feasts. In the whole enterprise, the central kerygmatic truths are to be preached on at the eucharist to elicit the response of faith, "whereas the aim of teaching [*didache*] is to secure understanding of the doctrinal, ethical and devotional implications involved in that response of faith".[16]

When God's Word comes to men at worship, it is both a divine and a human action. Robert Lechner refers to the "cultic Word". "The homily is also liturgy. Preaching within the liturgy is liturgy." [17] This means that it is not only worship proceeding from

[14] J. Murphy O'Connor's *Paul on Preaching* (New York: Sheed and Ward, 1964) is a study of the New Testament kerygma addressed to unbelievers. G. Wingren says there is no sharp distinction to be made between missionary preaching and the moral instruction given to believers: "When preaching proclaims Christ as the example of what the believer should be, it is dealing *with the world.* Christ dwells actively in his Word, and he is made flesh in the daily service rendered in the world by those who hear his Word and obey in their actions" (*Gospel and Church,* p. 30).

[15] R. Fuller, *op. cit.,* p. 43; cf. J. Dowdall, "Preaching and the Liturgy," in *Preaching,* pp. 26-40.

[16] R. Fuller, *op. cit.,* p. 53; C. Davis, *op. cit.,* p. 18, distinguishes between evangelization (*kerygma*) and catechesis which is "a deeper and more detailed presentation of the gospel message, with the purpose of nourishing the Christian life of believers".

[17] R. Lechner, "Liturgical Preaching," in *Preaching the Liturgical Renewal.* Instructional Sermons and Homilies, preface by H. A. Reinhold

man upward; it is also God's incorporative and formative action making the hearers into the living Christ who is forever at work in glory redeeming us.

Karl Barth, in a series of lectures first delivered several decades ago, discusses the behavior and conduct of the Christian preacher[18] and the great tension that occurs in seeking to be totally faithful to the biblical text while giving a meaningful talk to men of today.[19] In Newman's aphorism, "Nothing that is of yesterday will preach." Barth is faithful to the nature of a homily; throughout his treatment he does not discuss a sacred discourse or even a sermon. His chief principle is that the preacher must say in his own words what the bible says in the passage chosen for proclamation.

The *Instruction* of September 26, 1964, commenting on Article 52 of the *Constitution on the Sacred Liturgy,* requires that a homily explain some point from the day's scripture readings or from the text of the ordinary or proper of the day, "having in mind either the feast or mystery which is being celebrated, or the particular needs of the hearers".[20] This demand points to what is perennially the greatest problem of liturgical preaching: namely, relevance. Not many English-speaking Catholic homilists are on the alert to the existentialist interpretation of the *kerygma* asked for by men like Heinrich Ott.[21]

If God's Word and man must meet in the homily for the upbuilding of the whole Church—undue emphasis being placed

---

(Washington: The Liturgical Conference, 1964), p. 91. This small book contains a good, compressed statement on the precise nature of the homily on pp. 45ff.; cf. C. Gavaler, "Theology of the Sermon as Part of the Mass," in *Worship* 38 (March, 1954), pp. 205-07; G. Sloyan, Foreword in *To Hear the Word of God: Homilies at Mass* (New York: Herder and Herder, 1965), pp. 11-15. Probably the most complete summary of contemporary Catholic writing on the homily is W. Toohey, "Preaching and the Constitution on the Liturgy," in *Yearbook of Liturgical Studies* 5 (1964), ed. J. Miller (Collegeville, Minn.: Liturgical Press, 1965), pp. 15-28. Cf. also Vol. 1, nn. 1-2 of *Preaching: A Journal of Homiletics;* (Jan.-Feb. and March-April, 1966).

[18] K. Barth, *op. cit.,* pp. 43-55.
[19] *Ibid.,* pp. 75-77.
[20] Cf. *A.A.S.* 56 (1964), p. 890.
[21] Cf. H. Ott, *Theology and Preaching* (Philadelphia: Westminster, 1965), *passim.*

neither on the religious and human life of the people (subjective element) nor on the mere communication of a message (objective element)—proper balance will lie in the conviction of homilist and worshipers alike that Christ's resurrection for the redemption of humanity is the one saving Word that is relevant to men in all feasts and seasons. All homilies, therefore, are paschal. The preacher's task is to explore how this enduring relevancy can be made such in terms of a relevancy the worshiper will be aware of as he listens. This demands that the Word of God be spoken at times in the words of scripture, at other times in terms of the hearer's life situation, culture, vocabulary and needs. The homily transposes the Word of God addressed to all men into the Word of God addressed to this worshiping congregation.[22]

[22] A good example of the Word of God meditated on from liturgical texts is *Notes for the Preparation of the Homily,* prepared by a committee of twenty priests of the Archdiocese of New York (1966). In one sense all contained therein is relevant; in another sense none is yet relevant. For some problems of proceeding to the second stage, cf. Bishop J. Pike, *A New Look in Preaching* (New York: Scribner's, 1961). Two different approaches to relevance, the first staying close to biblical categories, the second transposing them to life categories more familiar to the hearer, are: K. Rahner, *Biblical Homilies* (New York: Herder and Herder, 1966) and H. Fehren, *Christ Now* (New York: Kenedy, 1966). The reader will observe that the above survey confined its attention largely to theoretical treatments, avoiding citation of collections of homilies.

Ludwig Bertsch, S.J./*Frankfurt, W. Germany*

German Literature
on the Homily

As regards the homily, understood in the strict sense of biblical homily, practical help for the preacher is not all that is available. There is in addition a wealth of other material, for the deepened awareness we now have of scripture's role in the proclamation of God's Word gives rise to the question of the precise nature of the homily.

Paul Wilhelm von Kettler (1852-1926),[1] the man who did most to further the fortunes of the biblical sermon in Germany, started a movement whose purpose was to reach beyond the history of the homily toward its definition and method.

Thus Fritz Tillmann's two-volume work *Die Sonntaglichen Evangelien im Dienste der Predigt erklärt* (Düsseldorf, 1917) was introduced by a summary of the history and theory of the homily written by A. Brandt.[2] J. B. Schneyer's *Die Homilie* (Kleine Schrifte zur Seelsorge, 13: Freiburg im Breisgau, 1913) was another attempt to nail down the homily's actual role and structure, and this too was preceded by an account of its original form and some historical examples of its use.

---

[1] Cf. particularly: "Zur Entwicklungsgeschichte der Predigtanlage," in *Tüb. Theol. Quartalschrift* 74 (1892), pp. 72-120, 179-212; "Die Lehre von der Homilie," in *Der katholische Seelsorger* 4 (1892), pp. 53-58, 105-13, 155-62, 260-69.

[2] This introductory section has been included in the new edition prepared by Paul Gödeke (Düsseldorf, ⁹1965).

In his own but most instructive manner, G. Fesenmayer, in *Bibelpredigt im Aufbruch, Versuche zur Erneuerung der biblischen Verkündigung* (Biblische Predigten 1: Freiburg im Breisgau, 1962), set out to demonstrate the genesis of the biblical sermon with a view to preparing the ground for the research he was to do for the subsequent volumes in the series, whose purpose would be to offer help of a more practical nature.

Efforts such as these are now being usefully supplemented by exegesis and through discussion between exegetes and experts on the homily.

Some important biblical studies and books on scriptural theology[3] are concerned with the clarification of the concept of the homily and of its specific function, as well as with research along similar lines that throws light on the direction of homiletic development.[4] Even if total agreement on linguistic rules is still lacking, all writers thus far mentioned are united in their acceptance of H. Kahlefeld's definition of the "biblical homily": "That it is biblical means that, be its approach thematic or exegetic, it is at all times faithful to those historical and supremely authoritative texts, and that it transmits to its audience the apostolic word as such."[5]

A comparison of the purpose of the previously mentioned works with A. Günthor's analysis of the homily in *Die Predigt* (Freiburg im Breisgau, 1963, pp. 68-72, 222-39) demonstrates that they are of service to homiletic practice as well as theory. In Günthor's book the homily, as an explanation of the Word of God proclaimed in the liturgy, is simply equated with the

[3] Heinrich Schlier, *Die Verkündigung im Gottesdienst der Kirche* (Cologne, 1953); *idem, Wort Gottes* (Rothenfelser Reihe, 4) (Würzburg, 1958); Wilhelm Pesch, *Der Ruf zur Entscheidung* (Schriftenreihe des Institutes f. miss. Seelsorge, 4) (Freiburg im Breisgau, 1964); "Wort Gottes," in *Anima*, 10 (1955), pp. 259-352.
[4] "Die Bibelwissenschaft des NT und die homiletische Ausbildung," in *Theologie und Predigt* (Arbeit und Berichte der Arbeitsgemeinschaft der kath. Homiletiker Deutschlands, 1, ed. by O. Wehner and M. Frickel) (Würzburg, 1958), pp. 132-41; 142-47. "Die Predigt," in *Anima*, 10 (1955), pp. 361-445.
[5] "Die Biblische Homilie," in *Exegese und Verkündigung* (Katholisches Bibelwerk) (Stuttgart, 1964), p. 23.

mystagogic sermon. This has the result of confirming the definition of the homily commonly accepted in France, which presents its true nature as something determined not by fidelity to scripture but by the constitution of the audience receiving it.[6] Clearly evident is the importance of reaching a clear definition of the homily that will also clear up the confusion in the practical sphere.

Practical concern about the homily has focused attention on another question: namely, the relationship between modern exegesis and preaching. Much has been written on the subject but first mention should go to Rudolf Schnackenburg's *Exegese als Zugang zur Verkündligung*.[7] The exegete's true objective— "to determine the meaning of scripture on the strict basis of direct reference to what was said by the biblical writer . . . to distinguish the pronouncements important to the faith . . . and to see how these fit into the totality of the early Church's Christian witness" [8]—is the unconditional presupposition of the biblical sermon. Furthermore, in the course of examining the texts with these aims in mind, one finds examples of that process so fundamental to biblical preaching: to acquaint the listeners through lively delivery with the words and deeds of the Lord, and to instill these in their attitudes toward life as divine realities so that they become beneficial to them.[9] H. Kahlefeld demonstrates this through five basic examples. However, their purpose, as he uses them, is not to serve as sermon guides to the texts concerned; he intends them primarily, as his final summary shows, to demonstrate through their role as exemplars the particular characteristics and significance of the biblical homily.

Through their contributions to *Anzeiger für die katholische Geistlichkeit,* A. Deissler and A. Vögtle have done much to open up important questions concerning the sermon and cate-

---

[6] For non-believers, kérygme = proselytizing sermon; for those under instruction, catéchèse = instructional sermon; for those taking part in the eucharist, homélie = homily or mystagogic sermon. Cf. *ibid.*, p. 70.

[7] *Exegese und Verkündigung*, pp. 7-22.

[8] *Ibid.*, p. 9.

[9] *Ibid.*, p. 21.

chesis.[10] There are numerous books that treat exegetical problems with an eye to the place of scripture in the religion lesson. Though they are helpful to a study of the homily, this article is not the place in which to consider them.

A series of articles in *Anima* 19 (1964), pp. 77-162, under the general title "Bibelkritik und Apostolat", offers a detailed study of the sermon.

In *Bibel und Leben* (Düsseldorf, 1960ff.), *Bibel und Kirche* (the journal of Katholisches Bibelwerk: Stuttgart, 1946ff.) and *Bibel und Liturgie* (the journal of the liturgical center in Klosterneuburg near Vienna, 1926ff.) we have reviews whose set program includes the idea of easing the transmission from text to sermon through printing articles on exegesis and scriptural theology and supplying practical bible study schemes.

Other series of books with the same purpose include the *Stuttgarter Bibelstudien,* edited by Herbert Haag, Norbert Lohfink and Wilhelm Pesch (1965ff.; twenty volumes to date); *Geistliche Schriftlesung* (Düsseldorf, 1962ff.) and the three-volume *Weg ins NT,* a commentary by G. Schiwy of which only the first volume (on Matthew, Mark and Luke) has been published so far (Würzburg, 1965).

There is also another group of publications whose intention is to present practical sermon guides, but they do it either by illustrating the passage from text to sermon step by step, or by offering basic examples of the homily in the form of complete schemes.

The first of these methods is adopted by the series *Am Tisch des Wortes* (Stuttgart, 1965ff.; fourteen volumes to date). The editors (monks of Beuron) and publishers (Katholisches Bibelwerk, Stuttgart) both allude to the two sources on which the renewal of the homily concept in Germany has been nourished over the last fifty years: the liturgical and biblical movements.

[10] Available in book form: A. Deissler, *Das AT und die neuere katholische Exegese* (Aktuelle Schriften zur Religionspädagogik, 1 (Freiburg im Breisgau, 1963); A. Vögtle, *Das NT und die neuere katholische Exegese I* (Aktuelle Schriften zur Religionspädagogik (Freiburg im Breisgau, [8]1966).

According to a fixed plan (liturgical and theological orientation, liturgical formula, epistle, gospel, scriptural theology, spiritual reading, meditation, proclamation) each book in the series proceeds to present a rich supply of material on the liturgy of feast day or Sunday. The wide extent of the material obliges the preacher to select from it whatever helps him with the sermon he wants to give.

Through limiting its material to just one of the two readings for Sunday or feast day, the bi-monthly biblical and homiletical journal *Dienst am Wort* (edited by B. Dreher, 1966) lightens the load on a busy priest without releasing him from the preparatory process altogether. The plan helps him to proceed from text to sermon in three stages (exposition, meditation, sermon scheme). However, the existence in each issue of many different authors sometimes makes this process more difficult than necessary. In both publications the greatest difficulty arises in the third stage where, after all, the ultimate object of the entire exercise lies.

Paul Gödeke took on an extremely difficult if not impossible task when he accepted the job of preparing a new edition of Fritz Tillmann's pioneering work (cf. footnote 2). Though amazed at Tillmann's achievement—his exegesis when he wrote the book nearly fifty years ago was in many respects ahead of its time—one misses some of the findings exegesis has reached since that time. Paul Gödeke could have brought these into his revision only if he had also rewritten the exegetical section. Because this was not done, his work in rewriting the other section was necessarily a more difficult process than it otherwise might have been. As if the difficulties he had with the section he did revise were not enough!

The only concern of the series *Biblische Predigten* (Freiburg im Breisgau, 1963ff.) is the outcome of the journey from text to sermon. "It is intended that well arranged matter of good sermon length will offer thought for meditation, point to the sermon and ease the burden on the memory. The preacher is left with the freedom and the necessity to choose his material." Thus did B. Dreher, the editor of the series, characterize its purpose.[11] A particular feature of this series is that the selection of scriptural texts is not limited to the liturgical ones.

Karl Rahner's *Biblische Predigten* (Freiburg im Breisgau, 1965; an English translation is in preparation) is a collection of some of his sermons, each of which is based on either the feast day or Sunday readings. Few of them are in fact biblical homilies in the strict sense, but the collection as a whole is a good demonstration that thematic sermons, as well as homilies in the strict sense, are needed to preserve a biblical foundation.[12]

[11] *Adventspredigten* (Biblische Predigten) (Freiburg im Breisgau, ²1963), p. 5.

[12] Limitations of space unfortunately make it impossible to include in this survey a mention of the considerable evangelical literature available on this subject.

Casiano Floristán/ *Salamanca-Madrid, Spain*

Spanish Literature on the Homily

The restoration of Spanish pastoral thought, in its biblical, liturgical, catechetical, homiletic, socio-religious and hodegetic aspects is in fact very recent. In the last ten years, a spate of pastoral books and articles has appeared—sometimes too many—mainly translations from French and German. Original Spanish works are still few in number, even though Spain is undergoing an intense apostolic renovation, led by nearly all the younger clergy and active laymen.

In Spain, it is obvious that the Council has produced a division between theologians with a long teaching tradition behind them and the present theological students, *au fait* to an amazing degree with translations of modern pastoral thought. And so, we live largely on imported thought. It is not easy to produce a good theological work in Spain at the moment without knowing several foreign languages, essential to follow what is being written in the Reviews, since few articles are translated into Spanish. Finally, the excessive number of seminary centers of theology (some 120, counting the diocesan ones and those belonging to the religious orders), coupled with the shortage of university faculties of theology (only three for diocesan clergy, not counting those belonging to the religious orders), makes the training of budding theologians for research and university lecturing extremely difficult.

Thus our young priests, seeing the urgent need for practical pastoral renewal and the immense field for apostolic work offered by Latin America, nearly all opt for pastoral work, even if they have just produced a brilliant doctoral thesis in some foreign theological faculty. And so, original Spanish works on preaching in general, or on the narrower subject of the homily, remain few and far between

A. A. Esteban Romero has provided excellent documentation on the theology of preaching and the debate on kerygmatic theology in his article "The Controversy over Kerygmatic Theology," in *XV Semana española de teología* (Madrid; C.S.I.C., 1956), and in his book *Predicación viviente al día. Una controversia teológica y una reacción pastoral* (Living Preaching for Today. A Theological Controversy and a Pastoral Reaction) (Madrid: Hogar Sacerdotal, 1956). Both study the origins of the kerygmatic debate and review the main works on the subject that had appeared up to 1956.

From the Argentine, J. C. Ruta has produced two studies on the subject, one an article, "The Theology of Preaching," in *Rev. de Teol.* (Buenos Aires, [1]1950), and the other a translation of Hugo Rahner's book on the same subject, *Teología de la Predicación* (Buenos Aires: Plantin, 1950). The present writer has also studied the theological problem of preaching from a kerygmatic angle and from the point of view of its relationship to the liturgy in "The Christian Kerygma. Concept, History and Controversy," in *Lumen* 6 (1957), and in "World and Sacrament in Pastoral Activity," in *Scriptorium Victoriense* 8 (1961). Finally A. de Villalmonte's *La teología kerigmática* (Barcelona: Herder, 1963) contains an excellent account of the kerygma and its theological implications. There are also numerous translations of works by P. Hitz, D. Barsotti, F. X. Arnold, Victor Schurr, Karl Rahner, J. A. Jungmann and others.

Approaching the subject from a biblical viewpoint, the homily has received profound exegetic treatment by J. A. Ubieta in his article "The Apostolic Kerygma and the Gospels," in *Estud. Bib.*

18 (1959). J. Apechera examines the preaching of the apostles in "The Biblical Bases of Preaching," in *Hodie* 4 (1965), and A. Torres the theological and biblical dimensions of the Word of God in "Word and Revelation," in *Burgense* 1 (1960).

El mensaje de los cristianos. Introducción a la pastoral de la predicación by L. Maldonado (Barcelona: Flors, 1965) is a book that has enjoyed particular success in Spain. It is a very thorough exposition of the content of the Christian message, or, if the old formula is preferred, a reflection on the essence of Christianity. The content of the message, centered on the death, resurrection and glorification of Christ, is studied through the four early forms of preaching: the confession of faith, the preaching of the apostles, the liturgical supplication and the *didascalia*. This is probably the most important Spanish contribution to the subject so far. Another excellent exegetic study, recently published, is *La Palabra inspirada. La Biblia a la luz de la ciencia del lenguaje* (The Inspired Word. The Bible in the Light of Linguistic Science) by Luis Alonso Schökel (Barcelona: Herder, 1966).

Among modern "aids to preachers" recently published in Spanish, first place must go to *Verbum Vitae. La Palabra de Cristo* (Madrid: Ed. Catolica, ²1955, 9 Vols.). As its subtitle indicates, it is an "organic repertoire of texts for the study of homilies for Sundays and feast days". It was compiled by a team under the general direction of the now Cardinal Herrera Oria, Bishop of Malaga. First published in 1953, and translated into Italian and English (considerably edited, under the title *The Preacher's Encyclopedia* [London: Burns & Oates; Westminster, Md.: The Newman Press, 1964-1965, 4 Vols]), each Sunday (in the English edition) is studied under six different aspects: scripture texts, general comments (liturgical and biblical), the Fathers, theologians, spiritual writers (including papal documents and historical and literary texts) and sermon schemes. This huge work has provided an abundance of material for preaching in Spain. Cardinal Herrera, with an authoritative and select team of helpers, has of course made an important contribution to evangelical preaching. But the whole work is too wide in scope for the average parish priest, though perhaps not for the theology student. Also, the biblical and liturgical considerations stand in need of considerable revision today.

Another Spanish collection which is a great help in preparing the Sunday homily is *Palabra de Vida. La homilia y el comentario de la misa* (Word of Life. The Homily and Commentary at Mass) (Madrid: Iris, ²1966). Compiled under the direction of T. Cabestrero, in collaboration with the Claretian theology faculty of Salamanca, it is in the form of separate studies for each Sunday and feast day, each divided into sections on the place of the feast in the liturgical year, analysis of the texts, biblical-liturgical theme, psychology and modern mentality, and guide to applications. It is accurately focused, both in its conciliar concept of the homily and in the help it gives the priest. Naturally, since each section is very short, its formative aspect depends on further reading.

Translations that help in the preparation of the Sunday homily include the eight volumes of A. Koch's *Docete,* subtitled "The Basic Formation of the Preacher and Retreat-Giver", although they are not as widely used as they were formerly. Much used now are the translations of the five volumes of *Guide de l'assemblée chrétienne* by Thierry Maertens and J. Frisque (published in English as *Guide for the Christian Assembly* by Biblica of Bruges) and of the collection *Assemblées du Signeur.* The translation of the latter has had a remarkable success.

On the more theoretical level, translations of E. Haensli's essay, "Preaching Today in the Light of Living Theology," published in *Panorama de la Teología actual,* eds. Feiner-Trütsch and Böckle (Madrid: Guadarama, 1961), which has been widely read by seminarians and young priests, D. Grasso's "Ministry of the Word Today," in *Problemas actuales de Pastoral* (Madrid: Sec. Nat. de Pastoral, 1963), and his recent work *Teología de la predicación* (Salamanca: Sígueme, 1966) have all helped to further the theology of preaching. *Hablemos de la predica-*

ción by G. Michonneau and F. Varillon (Barcelona: Estela, 1965) has also had an excellent reception.

Turning, finally, to original Spanish works on the modern concept of the homily, the major study by R. Rabanos, *Homilética Bíblica* (Lecciones de Pastoral, 9) (Barcelona: Flors, 1962) deserves recognition. The first part, the most original and best developed, is a history of homiletic preaching. The second deals with the homily in practice; this part is wide in scope and perhaps somewhat diffuse in treatment. The work as a whole is rich in information but lacks inner cohesion and a strictly liturgical conception. Another recent contribution is *Servidores de la palabra* (Servants of the Word) by a group of Dominicans (Salamanca: San Esteban, 1965). The writers study preaching in relation to the bible and theology, but they do not touch on the meaning and content of the homily, perhaps because the book does not seriously get to grips with liturgical considerations.

The essay by J. M. Setien, "Supernatural Technique of Preaching and the Homily," in *Orbis Catholicus* 5 (1962) examines preaching in general and homiletics in particular, proceeding systematically through the object, efficacy, aim, recipient, content and form of the homily. This is a valuable contribution to the subject, clear and yet profound, keeping biblical, theological and sociological considerations in focus.

There are several Spanish commentaries, most of them short, on the *Constitution on the Sacred Liturgy* and the *Instructio*. J. Camprodon, in his essay "The Priest as Minister of the Homily," in *Phase* 3 (1963), gives practical guidance on the long-term and immediate preparation of the homily. The article by E. M. Zamora in *Liturgia* 19 (1964) on "Different Forms of the Proclamation of the Word in the Constitution" is an overall exposition of all the aspects of the liturgy of the Word, including the homily. It has a good bibliography.

The homily as a liturgical action, biblical preaching and the explanation of the vital Christian message are brought together by B. R. García, in his article, "The Homily," in *Rev. Litúrgica Argentina* 19 (1964), by T. Cabestrero, "The Historical Trajectory of the Homily," in *Ecclesia* 24 (1964) and "Pastoral Problems of the Homily," in *Ecclesia* 25 (1965), and by R. Sala, "The Homily," in *Phase* 5 (1965).

I myself have tried in two different but complementary articles ("The Homily," in *Sal Terrae* 53 [1965] and "The Homily as Liturgical Preaching," in *Pastoral Misionera* 2 [1966]) to set out the concept of the homily as it can be deduced from the conciliar texts. The homily is seen as "a part of the prophetic ministry, liturgically sacralized, which proclaims the marvelous works of God in the history of salvation". The homily is preceded in the ministry of the Word by evangelization and catechesis. Basically the homily is *saying* (liturgically) *something* (a fact of salvation) to *someone* (the assembly). From this it follows that it must have three basic aspects: the Word of God (the biblical theme), the celebration (passing from Word to rite) and the world (realities of life). But since not all the members of the assembly are evangelized or catechized, there are three types of homily, each addressed to a particular community: the evangelizing, catechizing and mystagogic homily, each with its accent falling on a different aspect of the prophetic ministry.

Mensaje del Concilio (The Message of the Council) by C. Castro (Madrid: Cristianidad, 1966) is an original study of the homily, at once spiritual and religious. Perhaps the most thorough Spanish study of the subject is the second issue of *Pastoral Misionera* (March-April, 1966), devoted entirely to the theme of preaching.

Silverio Zedda, S.J./ *Chieri, Italy*

Italian Literature
on the Homily

W̲e shall first present two *studies* on the homily, followed by two books on *method,* and conclude with some *aids* to homiletic explanations. First place among the studies belongs to the book by D. Grasso, *L'annunzio della salvezza, teologia della predicazione (Historia Salutis,* Vol. I: Naples: D'Auria, 1965); cf. Eng. tr.: *Proclaiming God's Message* (Notre Dame: University of Notre Dame Press, 1965). The pages dealing with the homily are few but compact (pp. 325-28; 334-39; 360) and benefit by being included within the framework of a theological treatment.[1] The missionary preaching *(evangelization)* whose aim is the acceptance of the faith, the initiation into a knowledge of the faith *(catechesis)* and the liturgical preaching *(homily)* designed to quicken the faith already accepted and known (pp. 325-26) are among the forms of presentation of the message determined by the audience for which they are destined, or, better still, by the end in view.

This tripartite division corresponds to three phases in the relation with Christ: a first encounter, knowledge and a life in Christ (pp. 327-28). "The homiletic preaching prods the will to live in harmony with the commitments assumed in baptism and explained in catechesis" (p. 328); in other words, "the

[1] The author announces (p. 325) the publication of a future book in which he will deal more extensively with the various forms of preaching.

143

initiation into the mystery of Christ is followed by the life in Christ" (p. 334). The third form of preaching is characterized by the liturgical framework in which it takes place, for which reason it is reserved to the priest; it is a cultic act. Preaching "constitutes the liturgical signs in their nature as symbols of a suprasensible reality" and disposes the faithful "for the fruitful reception of the sacraments" (p. 355). "The homily is a means which the liturgy employs to accomplish its proper end—that is, the union of the faithful with Christ—so that in him, with him and through him they may offer to God the worship that is due him" (p. 335).

Nevertheless, the homily "is not reducible to catechesis" (p. 336) whose proper end is instruction. The homily leads to prayer and to the exercise of the theological virtues (*ibid.*). The other differences between the two forms of preaching derive from the different purposes of the catechesis and the homily. Catechesis is systematic, more didactic, calmer in tone, but it courts the risk of falling into the abstract, the abstruse, into erudition and polemics. The homily adheres more closely to the bible; it is more lyrical and dynamic in character, but it can fall into rhetoric, sentimentality and moralism (p. 337). The author concludes (pp. 337-39) that even though they are distinct, the three forms of preaching have several elements in common and reciprocally complement each other in pastoral life.[2]

The second study that merits mention is a work by S. Maggiolini, *La predicazione nella vita della Chiesa, lineamenti di riflessione pastorale sul problema della proclamazione della parola di Dio* (*Morale e Pastorale* I; Brescia: Editrice Queriniana, 1961). The entire fifth chapter is devoted to preaching at Mass (pp. 199-234). The importance accorded the subject is

[2] D. Grasso himself has written a book entitled *Evangelizzazione, catechesi, omilia* which treats of the three forms of preaching. For a terminology of preaching, cf. *Gregorianum* 42 (1961), pp. 242-67 (quoted in *L'annuncio della salvezza*, p. 339, footnote 16). The term homily is an apt one: it indicates an intimate talk addressed to the brethren to exhort them (cf. *ibid.*, p. 360).

immediately justified for two reasons: preaching during Mass is the most complete and perfect realization of the very concept of preaching, and it is the normal means for the formation of the Christian people in a community spirit (pp. 201-03). In the development of these two concepts, the homily is viewed as an integrating part of the liturgical action and not as a superfluous introduction to the "true" Mass (p. 204). Indeed, it is perfect preaching because of its origin and because of its purpose (p. 208); the sources of the homily are the life of the Church and the holy scriptures.

The Church is made visible in the liturgical assembly under two aspects; as a community of the saved and as a community with a hierarchical diversification; it is the birthplace of the perfect preaching which is the homily. Preaching will be listened to more profitably in the Church assembly gathered for the Mass because in the midst of that assembly there is a particular and active presence of God and Christ and therefore greater grace (pp. 205-08), and because Christ speaks there by way of authority: in the priest the believer listens to the Church speaking (pp. 208-10). Further, "one could say that the place of the bible as a source of preaching also has a visible presentation" in the Mass (p. 210). At the moment of the homily the assembly is already prepared for the action of grace through prayers, hymns and proclamation of scripture, and it is from this last that the assembly and the priest have received the object and the method of preaching itself (pp. 211-12). The homily, moreover, is ordered to the sacrifice of the covenant, and it is therefore an announcement of salvation effected by God in Christ, an announcement and proposal of the new covenant to be freely accepted, an announcement of the commitments that derive for the Christian people from the free acceptance of the covenant; therefore, the homily is not a marginal element of the sacrifice (pp. 212-16). Indeed, the homily is the normal means for the formation of the people so that it may endow all life with a sacrificial significance; moreover, it is not an inadequate means if it bestows what is *essential* along with the necessary insistences and nuances, and if the imperatives facing Christians and faithfulness to the liturgy are properly blended (pp. 217-18).

How then are we to understand and practice the pastoral duty of the "catechetica institutio" prescribed by the code (pp. 219-21)? The attempt that was made to replace the homily with the catechism suffered from different defects and drawbacks, above all, that of "inserting a doctrinal exposition in the unfolding of a rite of which no account was taken" (p. 222). It stemmed from the fact "that there had not yet been a sufficient intuitive grasp of the possibility of communicating revelation in its essential and sufficient entirety and its splendor through preaching conducted with reference to the liturgy and, specifically, with reference to the festive holy Mass (pp. 224-25).

There is as yet no sure and tested method for doing this (pp. 221-25). The author suggests that priests, whether individually or in groups, fix the themes of individual sermons in a plan that provides for a logical arrangement of the evangelical message. Therefore, the essential themes and their assignment to various periods of the liturgical year, in four- or five-year cycles, should be exactly identified by making the themes harmonize with the logic of the liturgical year—that is, by making the lesson themes arise from the liturgical year, from the major solemnities, from the unique themes of the individual Sundays or from the dominant one, since unity of theme does not always exist (pp. 225-28), while at the same time returning with greater frequency to the essential themes (pp. 229-30).

The latter considerations of Maggiolini's penetrating book bring us to the practical plane of homiletic preaching. Two works, now available in Italian, are found on this plane. The first, authored by G. Michonneau and F. Varillon, is *Rinnovare la predicazione* (*Nuova Predicazione* 3: Turin: Borla, 1965); original title: *Propos sur la predication;* Paris: Éditions du Cerf; cf. *From Pulpit to People* (Westminster, Md.: Newman Press, 1965).

The fourth chapter of the first part (written by Abbé Michonneau) deals with "parochial preaching". It contains practical advice (based on the experience of the famous Paris pastor), examples and points of departure for a salutary reflection on the duty of giving the homily, on the usefulness of preaching for the formation of the whole of the parish with "the whole of the doctrine" (pp. 67-69), and on the necessity of delivering a homily "at all Masses" (p. 74), even at those celebrated in the early morning. However, they must not be too long: "The length of sermons in certain parishes becomes a calamity" (p. 76).

Priests who must prepare homilies will find the second part of the book (written by Fr. Varillon) very useful, especially pp. 146-52 on the "non-utilization" of the bible, on the method of introducing the faithful into the biblical world and to the more profound meaning of the words (even without quoting Hebrew and Greek!), and on study unimpaired by the reading of the daily press, which "disturbs every form of silence" and which every morning "robs the priest of the purest moment of his day" (p. 151).

The second is an Italian edition (with a preface by Giovanni Colombo, now archbishop of Milan) of F. Valentine's book *The Art of Preaching* (London: Burns, Oates and Washbourne, Ltd.). It is a collection of practical suggestions for training seminary students of theology and young priests in the art of preaching; they are the result of psychological studies and broad experience. The book's comments on preaching in general, on proximate and remote preparation, on functional freedom and obstacles to it, on personal integration, on the use of the voice, on how to arouse interest and on how to conclude the sermon are very useful for the homily.

After the two studies on the homily and the two practical works on preaching in general which are also valid for the homily, we shall now present some *aids;* that is, developed homilies. The book by G. Paoli, *"Io sono la luce del mondo": i giorni festivi illuminati da considerazioni evangeliche* (*Pagina Sacra:* Milan: Ancora, 1962), is distinguished by an excellent analysis of human problems, using the evangelical text as a point of departure; exegesis and biblical theology are almost completely lacking. The book by A. Alberti, *Vangeli festivi* (*Pagina Sacra:* Milan: Ancora, 1963), is similar to the aforementioned work but it is richer in exegetical and theological references and presupposes familiarity with an exegesis already made in a previous work by the same author, *Orizzonti evangelici.* The two works are useful because of the hortatory reflections which are always welcome in a homily, but in our view they should come only in a second phase after the exposition of the text and of the biblical theme.

Excellent dogmatic theology is contained in the three notebooks on Sunday catechesis of the well-known writer and lecturer, Raimondo Spiazzi O.P.: I. *Avvento-Settuagesima,* II. *Settuagesima-Pentecoste,* III. *Pentecoste-Avvento* (*Temi di predicazione,* nn. 43, 44, 49, 50). They are outlines of sermons— "an attempt at catechesis" to be carried out during the Mass— which in the treatment of a theme adapted to the liturgical period very nicely arrange the texts of the Mass of the day—introit, epistle and gospel—in their true meaning, corroborated and explained biblically with the quotation of many other biblical passages.

We possess a true though brief exegesis of the Sunday gospel text in G. Cristaldi's *Parole di sempre, riflessioni sui Vangeli domenicali* (*Verbum Dei habeo ad te* 5: Pescara: Edizioni Paoline, 1964). After presenting the gospel passage, drawing for inspiration upon good books of exegesis and recent articles on biblical theology, the author relates the text to the spiritual needs of our time in a fresh and lively manner; it is a successful model of the fusion of exegesis and pastoral instruction.[8]

---

[8] We cite as generally useful for preaching "other Pauline editions" of books translated into Italian: Schurr, *Teologia della predicazione* (1962); Schlier, *La parola di Dio* (1963); Herrera, *La Parola di Cristo*: 10 vols. plus a volume of indices (1962-1966): Eng. tr.: *The Preacher's Encyclopedia,* 4 vols. (Westminster, Md.: Newman Press, 1965); Moeller,

The work of Ignazio Da Seggiano, O.F.M.Cap., *Esegesi teologica die Vangeli festivi* (*Verba Vitae*, Vols. 9, 12, 14, Treviso: Editrice Trevigiana, 1963, 1964, 1965), is richer in biblical theology. After a brief overall treatment of the gospel text, the author, a former professor of holy scripture, deals exhaustively, from the viewpoint of biblical theology, with a central *theme* that sheds light on the whole passage. This is followed by brief remarks of a pastoral character. Finally, the series *Meditazione e predicazione* (Brescia: Editrice Queriniana) merits special mention here. It consists of thirty small volumes which are most useful for the understanding of the liturgical periods of Sundays and feasts and for homiletic preaching (even when there is no explanation of the "readings", although explanations are beautifully provided in several cases). We shall list the most important of these excellent volumes, arranged in the order of the liturgical year:

F. Vandenbroucke, *Iniziazione liturgica;* H. Bars, *Dall'avvento all'ascensione;* H. Bars, *Dalla pentecoste all'avvento;* J. Mayer, *Un anno con il Vangelo;* A. M. Roguet, *Il tempo della speranza;* S. Grün, *Il Signore che viene;* G. Bevilacqua, *Omelie per l'avvento;* M. Cornil, *Meditazioni per l'avvento;* M. Cornil, *Meditazioni per l'avvento e il Natale;* P. J. Houyvet, *La prova del deserto;* R. Poelman, *Il segno biblico dei quaranta giorni;* F. Kolbe, *Verso Gerusalemme* (*quaresimale liturgico*); I. Laloux, *Verso la Pasqua, dalla settuagesima alla Pasqua;* R. Koch, *Prepariamo la Pasqua;* A. Löhr, *The Mass through the Year:* Vol. II, *Holy Week to the Last Sunday after Pentecost;* Valentin-M. Breton, *Nova via crucis;* K. Rahner, *Giovedi, venerdi santo;* G. Chevrot, *On the Third Day;* Y. Congar, *Pentecoste;* G. Chevrot, *Il tempo della Chiesa;* G. Chevrot, *Le domeniche d'estate;* G. Chevrot, *Domeniche e feste d'autunno;* F. Amiot, *History of the Mass* (translated by Lancelot C. Sheppard);

Mentalità moderna ed evangelizzazione (1964); Jungmann, *La predicazione alla luce del Vangelo* (1966). A. Ben's book, *Schemi per la predicazione delle SS. Missioni al popolo,* is brief but pithy (*Nuova Predicazione* I: Turin: Borla, 1963).

P. Biss, *I misteri di Maria;* A. M. Roguet, *Il credo, piano di predicazione inserito nell'anno liturgico;* D. Barsotti, *Introduzione al breviario;* G. Tansini, *Compieta, i salmi della sera;* J. Daniélou, *Holy Pagans of the Old Testament;* K. Rahner, *Encounters with Silence.*[4]

[4] In Italy there are certainly other works which would be worthy of mention. Those already mentioned here are works which have been made available to this survey through the kindness of publishers. In general, since it is impossible to review them individually, mention should be made of the homilies published in biblical periodicals such as *Parole di Vita* or publications intended for the clergy (*Palestra del Clero, Rivista del Clero italiano, Perfice munus, etc.*).

Gerard Hoogbergen/*Haaren, Netherlands*

Dutch Literature
on the Homily

We are still in a state where it is difficult to imagine that all those who have to preach regularly will make a thorough study of the relevant biblical passage one or two weeks prior to the sermon. Our clergy are not yet accustomed to the idea that the preparation of a homily demands *horae anxietatis et beatitudinis:* hours of labor in discovering the message and moments of joy because the discoveries are greater than the human heart can guess.

Nevertheless, there is great interest in the bible. There is a definite desire to link the homily with the passages read at Mass and therefore to refresh one's out-of-date biblical knowledge. There is a striking demand for a homiletic literature based on sound exegesis.

It is true that we can speak today of a biblical movement. The evidence lies in the many recent and valuable publications.[1] But in the matter of strict exegesis we are still lagging behind in our language.

In this article I shall first give a brief survey of the exegetical aids available; then I shall mention something about what has

[1] For a survey of publications that have appeared in recent years, cf. L. Hermans, "Uit de tijdschriften," in *Getuigenis* 9 (1964/5), pp. 145-56; V. van der Loo, "Kroniek van de bijbelbeweging in Nederland," in *Getuigenis* 10 (1965/6), pp. 56-63; E. de Roover, "Kroniek van de bijbelbeweging in Vlaanderen," in *Getuigenis* 10 (1965/6), pp. 150-69.

been written to help the preacher, and, lastly, something about collections of homilies.

1. *Exegetical Aids*

A preacher must first be helped with the meaning of words which, because of their Semitic origin, have a deep significance that the Westerner usually fails to grasp: desert, green grass, way, cloak, Jerusalem, etc. For this there are excellent publications in other languages.[2] In our own, we have a *Bijbels Woordenboek* which, however, seems to be more interested in the archaeological meaning of the words than in their significance for salvation.[3] One notices this when the treatment of key words like clothing, desert, and meal is compared to their treatment in French or German biblical dictionaries.

Modern exegesis penetrates still farther into the meaning of a passage through the results of historical examination of the style and genre (*Formgeschichte*) of the tradition (*Traditionsgeschichte*) and of the way in which the texts were edited (*Redaktionsgeschichte*). These results give us an insight in the way a biblical passage came to be shaped. This process was determined by the constant tendency to turn the material of facts and sayings into material for preaching. It was this intention to proclaim the message which guided the original community and the evangelists when they molded, selected and interpreted these data. To become acquainted with this development process means that at the same time one acquires indications for one's sermon. There is no lack of publications written with this in mind. Several periodicals contain numerous articles that study specific pericopes in the light of modern exegesis, as, for example, *Heilig Land,* which contains particularly good articles by B. van Iersel. *Tijdschrift voor Theologie* also contains some con-

---

[2] G. Kittel *et al., Theologisches Wörterbuch zum Neuen Testament* (Stuttgart, 1933ff.); J. Bauer, *Bibeltheologisches Wörterbuch* (Graz, ²1962); J. J. von Allmen *et al., Vocabulaire biblique* (Neuchâtel, ²1956); X. Leon-Dufour *et al., Vocabulaire de théologie biblique* (Paris, 1962). See also the "fiches bibliques" published by the review *Paroisse et Liturgie.*

[3] A. van der Born *et al., Bijbels Woordenboek* (Roermond, ²1954-1957).

tributions in this field, and there are many small volumes in the series *De Bijbel Over*. A manageable commentary is still to be desired.[4] This is shown by the impressive sales of the *Regensburger Nieuwe Testament,* which no longer satisfies the demands of the more recent exegesis.[5] For the gospels, in contrast with other countries we only have a commentary on the gospel of St John by H. van den Bussche.[6] In the series entitled *Het Nieuwe Testament* up to now only a commentary on Philippians has appeared, and in another series one on the first epistle of St John and one on Galatians.[7]

Finally, apart from the study of the words and the history of the origins there is still a third line which the preacher can pursue to discover the meaning of a pericope: namely, the literary form. Up until now this study has been neglected in regard to its being essential to the understanding of salvation, or it has only been appreciated as something accidental: as a vehicle for the content. But the succession of sentences and thoughts, the inner structure and the progress of the whole narrative are indispensable if we want to reproduce adequately the experience of the faith, as it was shaped in this specific way, for those who compose the present-day audience. The public reading of the pericope is in itself already proclamation.[8] The reader and the preacher are not tackling a dead text, but the reading and par-

---

[4] *De boeken van het nieuwe Testament,* by J. Keulers, though much used in the past, is now out of date.

[5] A translation by L. Witsenburg of the German edition by J. Schmidt and others of the Regensburger Nieuwe Testament (Regensburg, 1955ff.), which has been revised several times. The series will be completed by 1967.

[6] H. van den Bussche, *Het boek der tekens* (Tielt, 1959); *Het boek der werken* (Tielt, 1960); *Jesus' woorden bij het afscheidsmaal* (Tielt, 1960); *Het boek der passie* (Tielt, 1960).

[7] G. Bouwman, *De brief van Paulus aan de Filippiërs* (Nieuwe Testament; Roermond, 1965); W. K. Grossouw, *De eerste brief van Johannes* (KBS, Boxtel, 1963); *idem, De brief van Paulus aan de Galaten* (KBS, Boxtel, 1965).

[8] The importance of public reading has received special attention for some time by the institute *Ons Leekenspel* which organizes special courses to train priests in oral delivery. It has moreover made an excellent tape-recording of all the texts of the liturgy of Holy Week and has distributed this.

ticularly the hearing of the text is an event; it carries a call upon man, announces salvation and transmits the experience of faith and conversion. Such an analysis of the form in view of preaching was given in Germany, particularly by I. Baldermann[9] and was recently inaugurated in our language by M. Wilson and J. Streppel in *School en Godsdienst*.[10] It should be noted in passing that the appreciation of the form of a scriptural passage will not easily help the preacher in preaching about a specific theme. For this reason Baldermann is emphatically opposed to the "scopus" method, well known among Protestants, according to which the sermon does not rest so much on the scriptural passage as a whole (i.e., the homily), but rather on a theme, condensed in one sentence (*scopus*).[11]

2. Aids for the Preparation of a Sermon

Although the abbey of St. Andrew's, Bruges, belongs to our region and has for some years done some excellent work in this field of preaching, its publications are in French. The review *Paroisse et Liturgie* regularly contained articles by Th. Maertens in the period between 1961-1965 where he always gave a short commentary to help with the preparation of the homily.[12] Since 1962 these contributions have been given a separate and widespread publication in the series *Assemblées du Seigneur:* for every Sunday or feast there is a booklet, sometimes of 100 pages, commenting on prayers, sung pieces and readings, and this commentary is of a very high standard.[13]

The review *Getuigenis,* which deals seriously with funda-

[9] I. Baldermann, *Biblische Didaktik* (Hamburg, 1963).

[10] M. Wilson and J. Streppel, "Bijbelse didactiek," in *School en Godsdienst* 20 (1966), pp. 91-110. Cf. also B. van Iersel, "De bijbel van vandaag," in *'t Heilig Land* 19 (1966), pp. 18-21; *idem,* "De bijbel over . . . ?" in *'t Heilig Land* 19 (1966), pp. 50-52.

[11] I. Baldermann, *op. cit.,* pp. 46-50. Cf. also H. Kahlefeld, "The Pericope and Preaching," in *Concilium* 10: *The Human Reality of Sacred Scripture* (Glen Rock, N.J.: Paulist Press, 1965), pp. 39-51.

[12] For a full list, see *Par. Lit.* 47 (1965), pp. 853-54.

[13] Cf. Th. Maertens and J. Frisque, *Guide de l'assemblée chrétienne,* I-V (Bruges, 1964-1966). As preparation for the sermon this work is rather summary in treatment.

mental aspects of scripture and preaching, published (particularly in 1964-1965) a series of commentaries on the gospel passages for the Sundays of Advent, Lent and Eastertide which are most valuable for the sermon. In an expert way these authors provide a suitable biblical reflection for the homily.[14]

In the same way the "Work-Group" of Afflighem provided material for the homily on gospel passages in their *Dienstboek*.[15] It offers a choice of biblical texts around a biblical theme that stands out in the gospel passage. The contributions are sound and rich in suggestions for further biblical-theological elaboration. However, one may ask whether these suggestions pay sufficient respect to the passage as a whole. The central idea of a passage deserves attention, but in the gospels this is difficult without paying attention to the various details which the evangelists have grouped around this idea. It does not seem satisfactory to check the central idea as a key word in a good biblical dictionary. Such considerations of a biblical-theological nature are not special to a given passage but can be applied to many other passages that may have the same central theme.[16]

The bi-monthly review *Homiletische Schemata* provides sound instructions on the basis of an epistle or gospel passage. These instructions are not exegetical in the strict sense of the word, but rather biblical-theological, and they easily develop into more speculative reflections.[17]

The preparations for the sermon that have appeared since September, 1965, in the diocese of Den Bosch start from the idea that a contemporary and up-to-date exegesis is indispensable for the preaching of the Word of God. The contributions, by

[14] *Getuigenis,* a Review for biblical-liturgical piety (Roermond). The tenth year (1965/6) gives dogmatic-liturgical studies instead of exegetical ones.

[15] A. Verheul *et al., Dienstboek* (Antwerp, 1965).

[16] Cf., for example, Luke 5, 1-11 (4th Sunday after Pentecost). "At your word", the abundance of fish, the word of Peter (*kurios*—sinful), the water, "put out into the deep" and Luke's playing on the word "catch" —these elements, used to dress up the notion of "calling", have no place in a general treatment of "calling".

[17] Published by the Dominicans at Louvain in duplicated form.

some five exegetes and pastoral theologians, are put in the form of questions in order to stimulate personal study and team discussions in the presbyteries.[18]

3. Collections of Sermons and Reviews with Actual Sermons

It is not enough for the preacher to study the scriptures; he must start from there and then consciously address himself to his people by making the text acceptable and appealing to them. Every preacher will do this in his own way, and this the more easily as he has himself assimilated the message. Collections of sermons are useful for the preacher, not insofar as they lead him to imitate them, but rather insofar as they help him to overcome human inertia and stimulate him to a personal elaboration of the bible's message.

De Heer is met U, two volumes of sermons by L. van Herck, is an attempt to link the catechesis of the sacraments with the texts of the Sunday liturgy.[19] Since every year the same pericopes occur, it is possible to concentrate for one year on the sacraments. One may object that this method no longer deals with the pericopes in their own right, and the danger of introducing alien elements is not wholly imaginary.

A similar tendency to introduce such elements can be observed in the sermons which have been published in the review *Kerugma.*[20] Every issue has a motto (e.g., "ecclesial and non-ecclesial", "genuine living", "belief and unbelief") which is worked out in an introduction. This motto colors many of the sermons. Much care has been given in these sermons to a language that is concrete and intelligible. They are admirably adjusted to a contemporary audience. The ideas belong to this age, and there are several sermons that succeed in bringing out a sound homiletic approach to a given scriptural text. But in several others it is sometimes difficult to see what biblical text

[18] Published by the *Katholieke Bijbelstichting.*
[19] L. van Herck, *De Heer is met U.* Homilies about the sacraments (Antwerp: I, 1964; II, 1965).
[20] *Kerugma* (Hilversum), ed. by the Dominicans.

the author starts from. And so, one wonders occasionally whether God's Word or some human train of thoughts comes first here. Some sermons could be described more or less as an essay in popular theology, lined with biblical texts preferably taken from the epistle and gospel that have just been read.

The review *De Gewijde Rede* not only provides sound sermons for Sundays and feasts but also offers some good samples of sermons for special occasions (wedding, funeral, children's communion), for special categories of faithful (young people, the aged) and for a specific topic (prayer, marriage).[21] In recent years the Sunday sermons have usually been introduced by a brief exegetical explanation, sometimes formulated in one sentence (*scopus*). It is curious that readings from the epistles are so largely preferred to those from the gospels; this probably has led to a somewhat moralizing tone in some of the sermons. Preachers talk easily and a great deal to man and about man in an encouraging, friendly and sometimes over-cheerful manner.

The danger for the preacher of imitating and literally quoting such sample sermons is excluded without further ado from such books as *Lieve Gemeente* and *Binnen de Tijd* that have come out of the workshop of the poet-pastor, W. Barnard, who meant these works for use in any presbytery.[22] The same holds for the books of Th. Naastepad, *Op Water en Brood, Het Scharlaken Snoer, Op de Dorsvloer* and *Het Geheim van Rachel.*[23] These works of Barnard and Naastepad are gems of literary language and at the same time show great familiarity with the Old

---

[21] *De Gewijde Rede* (Malines), ed. by the Franciscans.

[22] W. Barnard, *Lieve Gemeente* (Amsterdam, 1961); *Binnen de Tijd* (Haarlem, 1964). The first book contains actual sermons, the second a rich collection of liturgical and biblical notices. In both books the author almost always follows the series of pericopes as given in the *Missale Romanum*.

[23] Th. Naastepad, *Op Water en brood* (Hilversum, 1959); *Het Scharlaken Snoer* (Hilversum, 1961); *Op de Dorsvloer* (Hilversum, 1964) and *Het Geheim van Rachel* (Antwerp, 1965). The collections reproduce evening services with sermons on passages, usually chosen by the author, particularly from the Old Testament (*Het Geheim van Rachel* is a series of sermons based on a continuous reading of 1 Samuel).

and New Testaments. They stir the imagination, provide encouragement for a truly biblical sermon and stimulate the personal elaboration of the texts. But they are limited precisely by their exceptional character. They are written by poets. Their very sensitiveness to language may appear to many as playing with words for the sake of the words, a conjuring with words, and their swift and surprising handling of texts from both Testaments indiscriminately as a nimble play of association of thoughts.

PART III
DO-C DOCUMENTATION
CONCILIUM

Office of the Executive Secretary
Nijmegen, Netherlands

M. C. Vanhengel, O.P. / *Nijmegen, Netherlands*

J. Peters, O.C.D. / *Nijmegen, Netherlands*

"This Same Jesus"

Writing on the dangers that could arise now that the Council is over,[1] Heinz Robert Schlette mentioned as a possible occasion of one of them the fact that the bible is now a subject of critical discussion among the laity.[2] As he saw it, this situation would be particularly dangerous if the resultant questions were either not answered at all or answered wrongly.

His fear has been justified. In April of this year, *Der Spiegel*, a mass-circulation German weekly, printed a detailed examination of the passion and resurrection narratives,[3] suggesting that what the gospels report about Jesus is full of inaccuracies, contradictions, anti-Semitism, etc.

The unsuspecting reader seems to be left with only one conclusion: the gospels are not trustworthy; thus faith has no reliable foundation. The articles (spread over two consecutive issues) do not merely attack the popular conception of the historical reliability of these narratives—an attack that could be justified—but they undermine the message of the Good News itself.[4]

[1] In drafting this documentation we have been helped by the advice and the writings of B. van Iersel, F. Theunis, E. Schillebeeckx and B. Willems; we planned it at a round-table discussion.

[2] H. R. Schlette, "Nachkonziliare Gefahren," in *Frankfurter Hefte* 21 (1966), pp. 613-14.

[3] W. Harenberg, "Jesus und die Kirchen," in *Der Spiegel* 16 (1966), April 4, pp. 86-109 and April 11, pp. 74-97.

[4] For a critical survey of recent literature see W. G. Kümmel, "Jesus-

This is a serious situation for which responsible Christians should show concern. It is being suggested that there is opposition between faith and history such as was formerly posited between faith and science. As a result many Christians are uneasy about the apparent conflict and one cannot put them off with references to Vatican Council II's statements[5] about the historicity of the gospels. That would be to ignore the seriousness of what is at stake. The way back to Jesus of Nazareth does not appear to be quite so obvious as we are inclined to suppose. Moreover, one ought to ask whether this uneasiness about Jesus in contemporary religious consciousness is not in fact due to causes other than those suggested by the people who suffer from it.

Therefore, this article will deal with (1) the nature of this unrest; (2) the legitimacy of the question about Jesus of Nazareth and possible answers to it; (3) the ways which, with the help of exegesis and other sciences, remain open for the approach to the Christ of the gospels; (4) the basic connection between the act of faith in Christ and the reliability of our information about Jesus of Nazareth.

I

THEY HAVE TAKEN AWAY MY LORD (JN. 20, 13)

The unrest described above is strikingly formulated in an anecdote about Bultmann[6] that tells how some worried readers and

---

forschung seit 1950," in *Theologische Rundschau* 31 (1966), pp. 15-46; for the philosophical background to these problems, see E. Castelli, *Mythe et Foi* (Paris, 1966).

[5] The *Constitution on Divine Revelation* of Vatican Council II mentions the *nuances* of truth "in texts that are in varying ways historical" (n. 12). Sections 18 and 19 point out the apostolic origin of the gospels and their historical character, and in doing so refer to the "Instructio de historica evangeliorum veritate," in *A.A.S.* 56 (1964), pp. 712-18; cf. E. Stakemeier, *Die Konzilskonstitution über die göttliche Offenbarung* (Paderborn, 1966), pp. 158 and 174-89. O. Semmelroth and M. Zerwick, in *Vatikanum II über das Wort Gottes* (Stuttgart, 1966), p. 46, refer to the concern of some fathers of the Council about what they called the arrogance of biblical scholars that must be restrained. Fortunately, Vatican Council II declined to do this.

[6] For Bultmann's demythologization program, see G. Hasenhüttl, "What

listeners used the words of the fourth gospel: "They have taken away my Lord, and I do not know where they have laid him", as a complaint to him about his demythologizing activities. One hears the same complaint from many people nowadays when, no doubt through a defective exposition of its aims, they come to hear of the results of modern exegesis. Where does this unrest come from? Certainly not just from modern exegesis, but rather from the fact that those who are thus disturbed have an exaggerated notion of the reliability of the documents, or because they have too crude a notion of the relationship between faith and historical knowledge. In other words it is their own misconceptions that lead them to ask too much of the documents available.

A good example of this was given by Anton Vögtle[7] in an article that should be read by anyone who is ill at ease on this point: "According to a popular preconception that bible historians have so far failed to eliminate, the gospels can only claim to represent the truth on all counts if everything to be read in them (other than items presented as metaphor or parable) is regarded as an official report of an event. . . . Thus every gospel event reported in narrative form must, to meet the requirements of this preconception, be understood as a chronicle, that is, as a description of an external process that actually happened as described."

To read the narratives about Jesus, as presented in the four gospels, with this kind of predisposition is to invite disenchantment. One then asks something of the gospels which they were never meant to provide, namely, a biography of Jesus of Nazareth. The gospels were never meant to transmit simple and straightforward information, but rather the Good News, which is most definitely related to actual deliverance and not merely to

Does Bultmann Mean by 'Demythologizing'?" in *Concilium* 14: *Do We Know the Others?* (Glen Rock, N.J.: Paulist Press, 1966), pp. 50-59 and J. Bourke, "The Historical Jesus and the Kerygmatic Christ," in *Concilium* 11: *Who Is Jesus of Nazareth?* (Glen Rock, N.J.: Paulist Press, 1966), pp. 27-46.

[7] A. Vögtle, "Die historische und theologische Tragweite der heutigen Evangelienforschung," in *ZKTh* 86 (1964), 4, pp. 396-97.

a liberating insight. We should not expect a kind of evidence that dispenses us from our own responsibility in the act of faith. The gospels are what a contemporary biblical scholar has called a "preached" history ("kerygmatized").[8] The adjective "preached" does not weaken the meaning of the idea of "history"; it indicates rather what kind of history we have to consider. Students of history should remember that historical interest does not exist in the abstract: one's interest is always concerned with somebody or something. In this case the interest centers on the message. Does this mean that the facts through whose narration the message is transmitted never happened? This is a secondary question, important but not the most important.

Perhaps all this will become clearer when we illustrate it in the light of a particular passage. The story about the storm on the lake is a good example. (Mk. 4, 35-41, but see also Mt. 8, 23-27 and Lk. 8, 22-25). Bornkamm[9] has already shown how Matthew has interpreted Mark's text, but Mark himself also helps us here.[10]

A superficial reading of the text might give the impression that a miracle is being narrated, accomplished by Jesus with regard to the elements, and that the passage is meant to show Jesus' power over the forces of nature. But this does not seem correct, because Jesus does not work the miracle while he himself remains on the shore. On the contrary, wind and water threaten the little boat in which he and his disciples find themselves. As all stories about miracles, this, too, speaks of the salvation of men.

But which men? Here we must distinguish between the narrated event and the manner in which Mark narrates it. The narrated event without doubt concerns the salvation that Jesus

---

[8] X. Léon-Dufour, *Les évangiles et l'histoire de Jesus* (Paris, 1963), p. 489.

[9] G. Bornkamm, G. Barth, H. Held, *Ueberlieferung und Auslegung im Matthäusevangelium* (Stuttgart, 1960).

[10] B. van Iersel, "Storm op zee," in *Het Heilig Land* 16 (1963), pp. 108-11. Another "kerygmatizing" interpretation may be found in X. Léon-Dufour, "La tempête Apaisée," in *Etudes d'Evangile* (Paris, 1965), pp. 153-81.

brings to his disciples. But is the narrating text concerned with the same thing? A small unevenness in the narrative can help us to find the answer. This unevenness lies in the curious place in his narrative where Mark puts Jesus' words: "Why are you afraid? Have you no faith?" (v. 40). If the narrative is a report, these words are definitely misplaced because the reason for the disciples' fear has already been eliminated. Therefore the verse would be much better placed before v. 39, so without doubt it is not by chance that Matthew puts it here (Mt. 8, 26). There is, then, every reason to conclude that Mark pushed it further away. And this has a twofold effect: The statement is better emphasized and, moreover, it is no longer really addressed to the disciples. To whom were the words directed then? There is only one alternative: Mark aims the words of Jesus beyond the disciples at his readers.

Once one sees this, other elements in the passage become clearer. Jesus' sleep and the disciples' cry: "Do you not care if we perish?" remind the reader, who is familiar with the Old Testament, of Psalm 44, 24 (cf. 107, 28). Brought almost to despair by persecutions, Israel fears that God has abandoned his people, that he is asleep, and in this mortal fear it calls on God to awaken and come to its assistance. Whether Mark wrote for the Christians of Rome or for those of Palestine, the community for which he wrote is recognizable in his gospel as a persecuted Church, and it is obvious that these Christians react as Israel did. Jesus promised his Church that he would stand by it. But precisely when the need is most pressing, we see nothing of this promise of help; it is as if he is asleep, as if he does not care that his community perishes. In this despair the evangelist sees lack of faith. And he addresses those who are persecuted and frightened with the words of Jesus: "Why are you afraid? Have you no faith?" And so the narrative of a miracle becomes in Mark the bearer of a message, a call to believe in the risen Lord precisely when in need, when one feels more than ever the need of his nearness, when the Lord does not make his presence a tangible one.

Mark, then, is concerned with this message. The question of what really happened remains. An answer is difficult. But the passage contains some details that are really irrelevant, such as the mention of other boats that went out at the same time (v. 36) and the description of Jesus being "in the stern, asleep on the cushion" (v. 38). With regard to the message, which is Mark's main concern, and even in the very narrative of the miracle, these details are loose remnants (particularly the mention of the other boats, which seems to reduce the scope of the distress considerably). But what are these details remnants of? At present we have to say they are remnants of memories. The picture of the other boats and particularly of Jesus asleep in the stern on the cushion seems to have taken such firm root in the memory that it rings out along with the message even though it has no significant part to play in it. As such, these details might therefore well point to something that really happened but which we can no longer reconstruct.

If this interpretation is correct, we do not have here the accurate report of an event. In Mark's preaching the event has lost its concrete limitation and has become a message for his readers, a message that can be made relevant for the readers of all generations to come.

To this we must add, of course, that the message has real force only if Christ is really referred to in the gospel. No doubt, it is not absolutely necessary that Jesus should have exercised his saving and liberating activity during his earthly existence in the way it is narrated. There is, nevertheless, no convincing reason why he should not have done so. On the contrary, for him who believes that redemption and salvation should become a reality for us today in Jesus Christ if we believe in the Good News, nothing is more normal than the conviction that God's redeeming activity assumed a far greater intensity in the person of Jesus than in the period that preceded him. The message of our salvation then appears to be based on God's saving act that takes shape in what Jesus does. This is also the reason why this message is proclaimed in slices of preaching that narrate what Jesus once did.

In the history of the passage analyzed above, we have seen how an event in Jesus' life has become the Good News. For the passage is not really concerned with the historical happening of how these disciples were saved from a perilous storm at some point in history, that is, insofar as it happened once in the past and can no longer be repeated in its concrete circumstances. First it uncovers the real heart of the historical event. Then, starting from this basic insight, we are taken beyond the historical limitation of the event to a transposition that makes this fact of days-gone-by assume an actual relevance for the listener. He then experiences in this preaching what Jesus is for himself.

II

BUT WHO DO YOU SAY THAT I AM? (MK. 8, 29)

To this question the disciples reply through Peter: "You are the Christ." Jesus of Nazareth is recognized and confessed by them and by the faithful as the Christ. He with whom we find contact in the gospels is Jesus of Nazareth as the disciples understood him and proclaimed him in their preaching.

This raises, spontaneously and rightly, several questions for the faithful of today.[11] Some of them are: What is the connection between the Christ in whom we believe today on the grounds of the Church's present preaching and the Christ of the earliest Church? This last question is really the way in which we justify our faith, whose norm is the Christ of the gospels but which must interpret him afresh all the time. We shall take up this question below.

Several biblical scholars have tried to answer the first question about the connection between Jesus of Nazareth and Christ. Searching for this answer is a process in which we actually participate, whether consciously interested or not, and we shall con-

[11] W. Marxsen, *Der Streit um die Bibel* (Gladbeck, 1965), p. 82.

tinue to participate in it. Historical research is not a soulless computer which does not involve us and which in time produces its punched cards that provide us with objective information. In principle, therefore, it is impossible to find an answer that satisfies everyone.

And yet, the question must be posed. Not to pose it is really escapism: either an escape into history, that is, into what is historically certain about Jesus of Nazareth, or an escape into a christology that ignores historicity. The mentality of the articles that appeared in *Der Spiegel* betrays an escape in the first direction, while contemporary theology is becoming acutely aware of the danger of its escape in the second direction.

Among those trying to find an answer we may distinguish two tendencies, leaving aside a number of *nuances:* (1) those who, with Bultmann, are convinced of the irrelevance of the historical Jesus. But it must be added at once that, although Bultmann helped the movement away from Jesus as a historical figure and as a historical reality and toward christology, he did so in such a way that he found him again as the historical Jesus who was preached; (2) those who want to raise the question about Jesus of Nazareth afresh—the New Quest.[12]

As far as the first group is concerned, Bultmann can see no continuity between the historical Jesus and the Christ of the kerygma, who is not a historical factor.[13] He does grant a link of historical causality and a kind of developmental relationship between Jesus' preaching and Christian preaching, in spite of an essential difference in content (*op. cit.,* pp. 17 and 22). As far as the historical Jesus himself is concerned, the Christian kerygma "is not interested in objective historicity beyond the *fact* that it happened" (p. 13). In other words: judged by the tendency proper to the Christian kerygma, this kerygma basically borrows from the historical Jesus of Nazareth only the mere fact of his

[12] J. M. Robinson, "A New Quest of the Historical Jesus," in *Studies in Biblical Theology* 25 (1959), and "The Recent Debate on the 'New Quest'," in *JBR* 30 (1962), pp. 198-208.

[13] *Das Verhältnis der urchristlichen Christusbotschaft zum historischen Jesus* (Heidelberg, ²1961), p. 8.

existence; it refers to this fact in asserting the identity of the
"event" of Jesus with the "event" of Christ that takes place in
the Christian preaching itself.

As to the second group, E. Käsemann[14] thinks that in looking
for the answer about the Jesus of this earth we should not yield
to skepticism and still less to a lack of interest. This would imply
that we implicitly abandon the original Christian conviction that
the glorified Lord is identical with the Jesus of this earth, and
this would lead to docetism (a tendency to consider the humanity
and sufferings of Christ as unreal and only apparent). Moreover,
the historian is able to recognize authentic sayings of Jesus in
the material that has been transmitted. For that reason Käsemann suggests this negative norm: statements that do not spring
from contemporary Judaism and cannot be identified as opinions
of the original Church must come from Jesus himself. For this
he refers, among other texts, to those where Jesus clearly assumes an unheard-of authority as in the contrasts between his
teaching and that of the Law (Mt. 5, 21f., 27f., 38f.) in the
sermon on the mount. This is reinforced by other texts such as
those where Jesus makes his position clear with regard to the
precepts concerning the sabbath and purity. Aided by these and
other texts that must be considered authentic, it is possible for
us to have some idea of Jesus' preaching and his corresponding
conduct. It is then also indirectly possible to say something
about Jesus' person, though not about Jesus' life in its outward
and inner development.

On the Catholic side, H. Schürmann[15] has attempted a method
based on positive norms. For this purpose he extends the application of the *formgeschichtliche* method to a situation in Jesus'
life which is certain, namely, the sending out of the disciples.
Many statements can be placed within this concrete situation
such as the fate of those who go out preaching and illustrations

[14] E. Käsemann, "Das Problem des historischen Jesus," in *Exegetische
Versuche und Besinnungen* I (Göttingen, 1960), pp. 187ff.
[15] H. Schürmann, "Die vorösterlichen Anfänge der Logientradition," in
Der historische Jesus und der Kerygmatische Christus (Berlin, ²1961),
pp. 342-70.

that Jesus himself taught them which they could use in their own preaching. This, in turn, would lead to important discoveries about what Jesus of Nazareth had in mind.

An answer is now also suggested to the question: "Who do men say that I am?", which is still a legitimate question. In the replies given to this question one can observe a certain convergence toward a continuity between Jesus of Nazareth and Christ. In the kerygma, it appears that we can distinguish a reality that preceded the rise of the kerygma contained in the gospels. We may call this reality Jesus of Nazareth with a scientifically satisfied conscience, but then also with that relativity which clings to any scientific knowledge. This relativity leads us to the third point.

III

BLESSED ARE THOSE WHO HAVE NOT SEEN AND YET BELIEVE (JN. 20, 29)

In the narrative of the resurrection, Thomas is told that to believe does not depend on an epiphany of Christ. *A fortiori* the biblical scholar cannot provide the disturbed believer with a "seeing" of Jesus that might serve as a substitute for faith in him. One can examine a certain gospel text in various ways. No text is ever without a certain scope for evaluation; it always contains in itself one or more possibilities of assessing it, or evaluating it. This holds true also for the writings of the New Testament. One can approach them as an example of post-classical Greek, or as a historical source for getting to know life in the 1st century, or as a source of knowledge for the historical Jesus, or as the expression of a new current in the history of the human spirit. Each of these evaluations corresponds to a kind of understanding and a special way of questioning, each with its own laws.

The evaluations we have mentioned are neither theological nor Christian but are common to any treatment of past texts. They exist, and nobody can do anything about it. Scripture, too, lends itself to all kinds of evaluations, to each of which corresponds a particular way of reading these writings. A theological, or more generally, a *Christian* use of the sacred writings is only possible in an evaluation of these books precisely as *sacred* writings: the Christian has received these books from the Church as an illustration which explains his *Credo,* as an aid for the Christian *celebration* of a believing *anamnesis* (commemoration), and so on.[16]

One way of approaching these books does not exclude another, nor should one way of reading them wrongly intrude upon another. The interaction of the various approaches is possible, often useful and sometimes inevitable. Thus the historical approach presupposes the philological approach; and the theological approach can be aided by the historical one although they should not be confused and the one does not provide the basis for the other. All this should be remembered when one finally asks what all this has to do with belief in Jesus Christ.

IV

I BELIEVE IN JESUS CHRIST

Belief is not a conclusion from observable data; this was already seen by the medieval theologians when they called the "light of faith" the only support for the faith. On the other hand, the content of faith is itself not a product of faith. The two tendencies which I described above as escapism are both rooted in the same presupposition, namely, that we know in a justifiable way only what is real in a verifiable and observable way. Anyone who demands this is bound to see faith either as a conclusion drawn from historically verifiable premises, or, when this historical investigation eludes us, as the product of purely human interpretations or something projected into the text.

Christ is not the great Presence in the life of the faithful because of the contribution which we make in faith. It is Christ's free gift of himself, accessible only in the faith, which called

[16] F. Theunis, "Hermeneutik, Verstehen und Tradition," in *Ermeneutica e Tradizione* (Rome, 1963), pp. 272-77.

forth the faith and the confidence of the original community, and so it calls forth our faith and our love. Christ himself is the Lord, the origin of the apostolic as well as our christological confession of faith *within* the situation of the faith, not beyond or outside it. It is not as if he is the origin only when we abandon any believing interpretation. God and man can never compete with each other. Christ's gift of himself determines the believing interpretation of the ecclesial community. We cannot prove the correctness of this experience and interpretation by the norms of a critical, scientific approach. This is a matter that concerns faith itself. When we look for historical facts in a historical manner—a perfectly legitimate approach—we put ourselves outside the approach of faith. And if we are troubled because historical investigation yields only a thin harvest, this trouble simply shows once again that we make our faith depend on historically verifiable premises: it is not a faith of unconditional *trust,* but a conclusion drawn from what we consider historical proof.

To believe, on the contrary, is a decisive, personal and total choice; it implies a certain self-understanding that can only be understood in the light of an unconditional surrender to God's infinite love for man. To believe is to entrust our whole being completely and unconditionally to that immeasurable love which Christ, living in his Church, promises us. This is what scripture bears witness to, and the same holds true for the Christians of the patristic age, of the Middle Ages, etc. And thus there arises a history of faith in which the always actual and unrepeatable (*einmalig*) call of the living Christ is nevertheless also always a *commemoration* of the other equally unrepeatable situations of faith which were experienced by our "fathers in the faith"; thus the faith remains open to the future. All these experiences of faith tell us: this *is* Christ. The first "deposit" of the Christian message of salvation, sacred scripture, is also addressed to us, even though it cannot be repeated in its concrete apostolic situation and as such is not directly relevant to us. But as addressed to us personally, a call aimed at our future, *now,* in our own situation, it touches the very heart of our existence.

There is, of course, also the point—which is beyond the scope of this article—that the trusting act of faith is a truly *human* act which, as such, must also be morally justifiable as a free act. Faith cannot be an irrational "leap" so that he who does not dare to take this "leap" would be just as right as he who does. Historical questions about the historical Jesus of Nazareth from "outside the faith" are clearly relevant, not insofar as faith as such is concerned but insofar as we are morally responsible for every human decision we make: in this case, the decision of faith.

BIOGRAPHICAL NOTES

PIERRE GRELOT: Born in 1917 in Paris, he was ordained in 1941 for the diocese of Orléans. He studied at the Institut Catholique in Paris, where he earned his doctorate in theology in 1949, and specialized in ancient Oriental languages. After being engaged in parish work until 1955, he taught sacred scripture at the Sulpician Seminary, and has been professor at the Theological Faculty of the Institut Catholique since 1964. His published works include *Man and Wife in Scripture* (1964). He has also contributed to numerous reviews, including *Revue Biblique, Vetus Testamentum, Lumière et Vie* and *Etudes*.

JOSEPH SCHREINER: Born in 1922 in Windheim, Germany, he was ordained in 1949. He studied at the Catholic Faculty of Würzburg and at the Biblical Institute in Rome. He earned his doctorate in theology in 1953, a degree in biblical studies in 1956, and was admitted to teach the Old Testament at Würzburg in 1960. He is at present professor of biblical history at the Catholic Theological Faculty of Münster. Among his published works in German is one on the ten commandments in the life of the People of God; he has also written many articles in biblical reviews.

JOSEPH BLENKINSOPP, S.D.B.: Born in 1927 in Durham, England, he became a Salesian of Don Bosco and was ordained in 1956. He studied at the University of London, at Oxford, and at the Biblical Institute in Rome. He earned degrees in theology and sacred scripture, and taught both subjects in England, the United States and Central America. At present he is engaged in scientific research on the Old Testament at Oxford. Among his published works is *The Corinthian Mirror* (1964), as well as numerous articles in biblical and theological reviews.

RAYMOND TOURNAY, O.P.: Born in 1912 in Paris, he became a Dominican and was ordained in 1936. He studied at the University of Louvain, the Ecole des Hautes Etudes and the Collège de France in Paris. He earned degrees in theology and sacred scripture, and taught at the Dominican House of Studies at Saulchoir and at the Institut Catholique in Paris. Since 1945 he has been professor of Old Testament exegesis at l'Ecole Biblique in Jerusalem. His many published works in French are on biblical subjects.

FRANS NEIRYNCK: Born in 1927 in Wingene, Belgium, he was ordained in 1953 for the diocese of Bruges. He studied at Louvain, obtaining degrees in philosophy and earning his doctorate in theology in 1957. He taught at the major seminary of his diocese, and is at present professor at the University of Louvain. He has published articles and contributed to collective works.

JOSEPH FITZMYER, S.J.: Born in 1920 in Philadelphia, he became a Jesuit and was ordained in 1951. He studied at Loyola University in Chicago, the Jesuit Faculty at Louvain, Johns Hopkins University in Baltimore and the Biblical Institute in Rome. He earned his doctorate in theology in 1956 and a degree in sacred scripture in Rome in 1957. He has taught in Baltimore and at the University of Pennsylvania, and at present is professor of New Testament studies at Woodstock College in Maryland. His published works include *An Introductory Bibliography for the Study of Scripture* in collaboration with G. Glanzman (1961), and *The Genesis Apocryphon of Qumran Cave I* (1966). He is a contributor to such reviews as *Theological Studies* and *Catholic Biblical Studies*.

DAVID STANLEY, S.J.: Born in 1914 in the United States, he became a Jesuit and was ordained in 1946. He studied at the University of St. Louis, and earned his doctorate in sacred scripture at the Biblical Institute in Rome in 1952. He is professor of New Testament studies at Regis College, Willowdale, Canada, and at the University of Iowa. His published works include *The Church in the New Testament,* and numerous contributions to reviews such as *Biblica, Theological Studies, Catholic Biblical Quarterly, Worship* and *Scripture.*

JULES CAMBIER, S.D.B.: Born in 1915 in Belgium, he became a Salesian of Don Bosco and was ordained in 1944. He studied philosophy and letters at the University of Louvain, and earned his doctorate in theology in 1948. Since then he has been professor of exegesis at the Salesian House of Studies in Belgium, and professor at the Theological Faculty of Lovanium (Congo). Among his published works in French are numerous articles in such reviews as *Revue Biblique, Diction. de la Bible Supplément, Irénikon, New Testament Studies, Biblica, Lumière et Vie, Assemblée du Seigneur* and *Revue d'Histoire Ecclésiastique.*

THIERRY MAERTENS: Born in 1921 in Huy, Belgium, he was ordained in 1946. He studied history, law and theology at the Universities of Liège and Louvain. He is editor of *Paroisse et Liturgie,* and has published more than 150 articles and over 40 booklets on pastoral, liturgical and biblical subjects. Among his published works is the five-volume *Initiation des enfants à la Liturgie.*

GERARD S. SLOYAN: Born in 1919 in New York, he was ordained in 1944 for the diocese of Trenton. He studied at Seton Hall University, earning a degree in theology in 1944 and his doctorate in philosophy in 1948. A liturgist of renown, he has been since 1957 head of the department of religious education at the Catholic University of America in Washington. Among his published works are *Shaping the Christian Message* (1958) and *To Hear the Word of God: Homilies at Mass* (1965). He is a frequent contributor to *Worship, The Catholic Biblical Quarterly* and *Religious Education.*

LUDWIG BERTSCH, S.J.: Born in 1929 in Frankfurt, Germany, he became a Jesuit and was ordained in 1956. He earned his doctorate in theology in 1960 at the University of Innsbruck. At present he teaches pastoral theology and homiletics. Among his published works in German are articles and contributions to collective works.

CASIANO FLORISTÁN: Born November 4, 1926, in Arquedas, Spain, he was ordained in 1956 for the diocese of Pamplona. He pursued his studies at the Pontifical University of Salamanca, at Innsbruck and at Tübingen, earning his doctorate in theology from the University of Tübingen in 1959. At present he is professor of pastoral theology and liturgy at Salamanca and director of the Pastoral Theology Institute there. His published works in Spanish deal with liturgical and pastoral subjects.

SILVERIO ZEDDA, S.J.: Born in 1913 in Gesturi, Italy, he became a Jesuit and was ordained in 1940. He studied at the Biblical Institute in Rome, and earned his doctorate there in 1952. At present he is professor of sacred scripture at the Theological Faculty in Chieri, Italy, and is also vice-president of the Italian Biblical Association. Among his published works in Italian are books and articles on biblical subjects.

GERARD HOOGBERGEN: Born in 1927 in 's-Hertogenbosch, Netherlands, he was ordained in 1957. He studied at the Catholic University at Nijmegen, where he obtained a degree in theology in 1960. He pursued his studies at the Catechetical Institute in Paris, and is presently teaching homiletics and catechetics in the major seminary of his diocese and a member of a group of exegetes that regularly publishes material for homilies under the auspices of the Katholieke Bijbelstichting.

Subject Index to CONCILIUM (Volumes 11-20)

FIGURES IN BOLD FACE INDICATE VOLUME NUMBER
WITH PAGE REFERENCES IN LIGHT FACE

Arianism, and the Fathers of the Church, (11) 114; and religious freedom in the early Church, (18) 7

Aristotle, theology of the soul in, (11) 152

Arntz, Joseph, O.P., (16) 179; on theology and modern warfare, (15) 120

Aron, Raymond, on communism, (16) 7

Arrupe, Pedro, S.J., on dialogue, (13) 70

Arseniev, Nicholas, on the *Constitution on the Church*, (14) 142-144

Artajo, A. Martin, on proselytism in Spain, (18) 99-100; on religious freedom in Spain, (18) 104-105

Ascension, Bultmann's interpretation of the, (14) 55; significance of the, (11) 74

Ascesis, necessity of, (19) 103

Asceticism, modern, (19) 100-108; Thomistic system of, (15) 60

Ascetics, eucharistic devotion of, (14) 170

Asia, liturgical renewal in, (12) 133-138

Athanasius, St., and Eastern ecclesiology, (14) 71; on the Holy Spirit, (14) 75; on religious freedom, (18) 6; on revelation and ontology, (11) 19, 21

Atheism, caricatures of Christianity in, (16) 110; in Communist ideology, (16) 159-160; contemporary, (19) 97; critical, (16) 123-125; in Freudian psychoanalysis, (16) 59-72; Marxist, (16) 7-24, 27; of Merleau-Ponty, (16) 41-47; negative, (16) 121-123; philosophical possibility of, (16) 111-128; positive, (16) 125-128; and the proclamation of God, (16) 89-98; relativity of, (16) 37; of J.-P. Sartre, (16) 41-47; scriptural meaning of, (16) 90f.; threefold possibility of, (16) 121-128

Athenagoras I, joint declaration with Paul VI, (17) 174-176; meeting with Paul VI, (14) 118; on the relationship between Churches, (14) 61

Aubert, Roger, (19) 184; on religious freedom, (18) 123; on the Vatican, (17) 14

Auctorem fidei, (17) 48-49

Aufderbeck, Hugo, (12) 174

Augsburg, peace of, (18) 12

Augustine, St., and Anglican succession, (14) 77-78; on the city of God, (15) 54; and Gregorian reform, (17) 74; and Luther's theology, (14) 13-15, 25; on music, (12) 50, 62; on the psalms, (14) 15; on religious freedom, (18) 6, 44; on the two cities, (17) 53-55

Australia, Church music in, (12) 127-130; liturgical renewal in, (12) 139-142

Authority, ecclesiastical, (15) 71-87; Anglican concept of, (14) 79-80; in Calvin's theology, (14) 33, 41

Authority, parental, in Freudian psychoanalysis, (16) 65

Avignon papacy, (17) 131, 159-160

Bainton, Roland, (15) 161; on American Protestantism, (14) 90; on war and peace, (15) 107

Bamberger, John, O.C.S.O., (16) 180

Baptism, administration of, (17) 45; and the concept of the laity, (13) 140; ecumenical notion of, (14) 116; eschatological aspect of, (14) 165; in the Free Churches, (14) 96-97; and the liturgical assembly, (12) 10; as a sacramental bond of unity, (12) 27

Baptismal font, and the liturgical assembly, (12) 42

Baptists, on the adult commitment of faith, (14) 96

Baron, R., on Catholic life in Communist China, (13) 57

Barraclough, Geoffrey, on contemporary history, (17) 9

Barth, Karl, and Calvinism, (14) 30, 35-36; christological approach of, (11) 24; (14) 43ff.; on ecumenical methodology, (14) 43; and ecumenical triumphalism, (14) 49; eschatological vision of, (14) 43ff.; on the Evangelical Churches, (14) 45; the fideism of, (11) 40; on the homily, (20) 129; on idolatry, (16) 109; on Luther, (17) 50; on *Pacem in terris,* (14) 49; and Protestant self-criticism, (14) 44-45; on religious freedom, (18) 56; and Vatican Council II, (14) 47-49

Basil, St., on the liturgy, (14) 168-169

Bonnefoy, Jean-François, on Christ's theological primacy, (11) 117-118

Bosc, Jean, (14) 177; on the *Decree on Ecumenism,* (14) 122

Boublik, V., on Christ's primacy, (11) 118

Bouëssé, Humbert, on Christ's humanity, (11) 117

Bouillard, Henri, on Barth's theology, (14) 43

Bourke, Joseph, O.P., (11) 161

Boylan, Eugene, (19) 146

Bramao, Luis, on population problems, (15) 49-50, 158

Bramson, L., on war, (15) 106

Brandenburg, Albert, on Luther's theology, (14) 15

Brothers of the Virgin of the Poor, (19) 175-182

Brown, Robert McAfee, on the *Decree on Ecumenism,* (14) 121, 124; on the obstacles to ecumenical dialogue, (14) 129; on religious liberty, (14) 101

Brunetière, F., on Calvin's rationalism, (14) 38

Brunner, Paul, S.J., (12) 175

Buddhism, (19) 159, 161ff., 169, 172, 174

Bühlmann, Walbert, O.F.M.Cap., (13) 151

Bultmann, R., on christology, (11) 109-110, 113-114; on Christ's ascension, (14) 55; on Christ's descent into hell, (14) 55; critical evaluation of, (11) 32-46, 58-59; (14) 52-53; and demythologization, (11) 37-42; (14) 50, 59; (16) 96; existential theology of, (14) 36; on the historical Jesus, (20) 168-169

Bultot, Robert, (19) 182

Buonaiuti, Ernesto, and the Italian modernist movement, (17) 103

Buri, F., on mythology in the bible, (14) 56

Bürkle, Horst, on the cosmic Christ, (11) 126n.

Byzantine churches, liturgical celebration in, (14) 171

Byzantine Empire, Church-State relations in the, (18) 148-150

Byzantine theology, and the Real Presence, (14) 173

Callistus, Nicephorus, on the remains of sacred species, (14) 174

Calumny, in missionary proselytism, (14) 105

Calvin, John, on Christ's descent into hell, (11) 155; and present-day Catholicism, (14) 27-41

Cambier, Jules, S.D.B., (20) 175

Cameroon, interdenominational organization in, (13) 44

Camus, Albert, on evolutionary humanism, (16) 56; on theology, (16) 3

Canada, liturgical renewal in, (12) 157-166

Canon law, and the bible, (17) 74; and Roman law, (17) 47-48

Canon of the Mass, significance of the, (12) 138

Capitalism, exploitation in, (15) 68; in Latin-American development, (15) 44f.; and morality, (15) 63-64; and pluralism, (16) 173

Cappadocians, and Eastern ecclesiology, (14) 71

Carnesecchi, Pietro, decapitation of, (15) 17

Cassian, John, (19) 48f.

Castellion, Sebastian, on freedom of conscience, (18) 14-15

Catechetics, in Africa, (12) 144; (13) 37-39; and mission, (13) 110; modern renewal in, (11) 6, 15, 23-24

Catechism, Japanese, (19) 168

Catherine of Siena, St., on the eschatological dimension of Pentecost, (14) 73-74

Catholic Action, in the African Church, (13) 42-43; misinterpretations of, (13) 143-144; and missiological revival, (13) 83-84; in the modern world, (13) 95-98

CELAM, (12) 153-154

Cerfaux, L., on the liturgical assembly, (12) 4; on the term "Son of God", (11) 12n., 13

Cerularius, Michael, reply to the bull of Cardinal Humbert by, (17) 173; schism of, (17) 155-169

Chandran, J. R., on the *Decree on Ecumenism,* (14) 121; on sin, (14) 123

Chandrasekhar, S., on overpopulation, (15) 149

Chang, Lit-Sen, works of, (13) 73

Charisms, in Calvin's theology, (14) 41; among the laity, (13) 142-143;

genre of the bible, **(14)** 51; new liberties granted in, **(11)** 5

Dix, Gregory, on the liturgical assembly, **(12)** 12, 17

Docetism, influence of, **(11)** 45

Dodd, C. H., on the homily, **(20)** 125-126; on the Petrine discourses, **(20)** 88

Dogma, priorities in, **(14)** 125

Dogmatic formulas, dynamic nature of, **(14)** 160

Dogmatic theology, Christ's kingship in, **(11)** 116-127; limbo and purgatory in, **(11)** 158; problem of Christ's knowledge in, **(11)** 91-105; structure of reality in, **(11)** 25

Dogmatism, present modification of, **(13)** 90

Domentianus, on the nature of orthodoxy, **(17)** 79-80

Domoulin, H., **(19)** 157f., 174

Donatism, in medieval theology, **(17)** 125

Dostoievski, Fyodor, on the Christian attitude, **(15)** 66; and religious freedom, **(18)** 142-143

Doumith, M., on religious freedom, **(18)** 141

Dournes, J., missionary theology of, **(13)** 117

Doxologies, dogmatic content of, **(11)** 10

Dreams, Freud's theory of, **(16)** 61-62, 73

Drums, in Church music, **(12)** 114

D'Souza, Eugene, on the Church's missionary task, **(13)** 5

Dubarle, D., on theology and modern warfare, **(15)** 125

Duméry, H., on the bible, **(19)** 61

Dunne, George, S.J., on population problems, **(15)** 147

Du Plessis, Isak, on cosmic christology, **(11)** 110-111

Dupont, D., on poverty in the New Testament, **(15)** 55

Dupont, J., on the Logos, **(11)** 10

Duquoc, Christian, O.P., **(19)** 183

Dutch literature, on the homily, **(20)** 151-158

Dynamic evolution, concept of, **(11)** 122-123; ultimate goal of, **(11)** 141

Earthly realities, theology of, **(19)** 44-58

Eastern Churches, and religious freedom, **(18)** 140ff., 157-161

Eastern cosmology, and Christ's kingship, **(11)** 110; mythical nature of, **(11)** 115

Ebeling, Gerhard, on Luther's theology, **(14)** 15

Ecclesia, meaning and use of the term, **(12)** 5, 7-9, 17

Ecclesiam suam, on atheistic communism, **(13)** 67-68; on missionary activity, **(13)** 74; on poverty in Christian life, **(15)** 56; on the relationship of the Church to Christ, **(17)** 146; on revelation, **(11)** 10; on the separated Churches, **(14)** 129

Ecclesiastical government, problems of, **(15)** 86

Ecclesiastical obedience, and eternal law, **(15)** 75ff.

Ecclesiology, in Calvin's theology, **(14)** 32, 36; Christ's kingship in, **(11)** 133; and christocentrism, **(14)** 32; in the *Constitution on the Church,* **(14)** 144-145, 148-149; Eastern, **(14)** 71f.; and ecumenical dialogue, **(14)** 67-68; expansion of, **(19)** 57; historical dimension of, **(13)** 94-95; and the liturgical assembly, **(12)** 34, 37f.; and liturgy, **(17)** 40-43; in the Middle Ages, **(17)** 122ff.; mission as a theme of, **(13)** 81-130; and pastoral problems, **(13)** 83-85; and redemption, **(11)** 159; and Vatican Council II, **(14)** 139ff.

Economic power, abuse of, **(15)** 44

Economic resources, and population problems, **(15)** 155-156

Economic welfare, and human dignity, **(16)** 36

Economics, and missiology, **(13)** 95, 102

Economy of salvation, Christ in the, **(11)** 5-25

Ecumenical conferences, on Christ's kingship, **(11)** 135-143

Ecumenical council, in the Orthodox Church, **(14)** 136; as a visible expression of the Church, **(11)** 134

Ecumenical dialogue, and the Anglican communion, **(14)** 77-85; basic aspects of, **(14)** 62, 118; and biblical theology, **(14)** 80-81; and Calvin, **(19)** 34ff.; and collegiality, **(14)** 64; communal aspect of, **(14)** 122; and ecclesiology, **(14)** 67-68; and epicle-

Human body, mutilation of the, (15) 92-94; and the principle of totality, (15) 91-94

Human conscience, and religious freedom, (18) 4, 14ff.

Human consciousness, dimensions of, (11) 103; of Jesus Christ, (11) 91-96; and metaphysical personality, (11) 96; psychology of, (11) 95

Human desire, and culture, (16) 62

Human dignity, and economic deliverance, (16) 36; in the natural law, (16) 36; and religious freedom, (18) 38, 43-47, 128

Human existence, final biological triumph of, (11) 82-87; modern reflections on, (11) 14-15; (16) 99ff.; and psychoanalysis, (16) 61f.

Human freedom, in Sartre's philosophy, (16) 42ff.

Human institutions, and transcendent faith, (14) 109-110

Human nature, and ecclesiastical obedience, (15) 75; ontological oneness of, (15) 116

Human organisms, and the principle of totality, (15) 91-94, 98

Human person, dignity of the, (15) 3ff., 18-19, 95

Human society, contemporary Christian view of, (14) 10; and the liturgical assembly, (12) 37-43

Humani generis, on mythology in scripture, (14) 51

Humanism, atheistic, (19) 67; and communism, (16) 12; eschatological, (16) 25-40; evolutionary, (16) 49-58; Marxist, (16) 11ff.; (19) 64; total, (16) 157-176

Humbert, Cardinal, bull of, (17) 170-173; and the schism of Michael Cerularius, (17) 155-169

Huss, Jean, recent historical research on, (17) 123ff.

Huxley, Julian, evolutionary humanism of, (16) 49-58; on overpopulation, (15) 146

Huxley, Thomas, agnostic ideology of, (16) 50

Hypocrisy, in Marxist philosophy, (16) 22-23

Hypostatic union, and Christ's descent into hell, (11) 156; in Luther's theology, (14) 19; and the soul of Jesus, (11) 94ff.

Idolatry, and atheism, (16) 124; sources of, (16) 109

Ignatius of Antioch, St., on Christ's human consciousness, (11) 64; on the eucharist, (17) 29-30; on the liturgical assembly, (12) 11-12, 14, 16, 18, 79; on mental obedience, (15) 77; on the presbyteral colleges, (17) 25-27

Illuminati, (19) 6, 28

Illusion, Freudian theory of, (16) 64ff., 73-88

Images, revelation of God in, (11) 9

Immaculate Conception, and the Orthodox Church, (14) 135

Immanence, transcendence opposed to, (19) 62

Imperialism, in Latin America, (15) 33

Incarnation, cosmological and ontological dimensions of the, (11) 107-127; and eschatology, (13) 94; and Marxism, (16) 14-17; missiological concept of, (13) 93f.; theological significance of, (13) 97; (14) 57-58; and transcendence, (19) 63

Incarnationalism, excess of, (19) 64f.

Incest, in Freudian psychology, (16) 77f.

India, death rate in, (15) 62; the hierarchy in, (13) 14; missionary action in, (13) 123-124; religious pluralism in, (15) 24; ritual in, (12) 135

Individualism, in Christianity, (12) 143; in the local congregation, (14) 99-100; in Protestant piety, (16) 145; in the West, (15) 115

Indonesia, Church music in, (12) 119-125

Indulgences, in Luther's theology, (14) 17; and the Synod of Pistoia, (17) 43-44, 46

Industrialization, and missiology, (13) 95f.

Infallibility, in Calvin's theology, (14) 32-33; and ecclesiastical authority, (15) 72-73; and Vatican Council I, (17) 137

Inhibition, in Freudian psychoanalysis, (16) 62; and religion, (16) 71-72

Innocent III, Pope, on Church-State relations, (18) 148; on marriage, (18) 170

Innocent XI, Pope, on the missions, (13) 19, 21

Inoue, Y., on the Westernization of Japan, (19) 160f., 163f., 169f.

Institution, in Calvin's thought, (14) 32-33; sociological notion of, (13) 125-127

Institutionalism, in the Church, (13) 85; and the idea of mission, (13) 113-114; in the post-Tridentine Church, (17) 41-42

Instruction on the Sacred Liturgy, reactions to the, (12) 83-91

Integritas, meaning of, (11) 59-60

Irenaeus, St., on the dignity of man, (15) 20; on the divinity of Christ, (11) 19; on presbyteral colleges, (17) 27

Irenicism, and the *Decree on Ecumenism*, (14) 124

Iron Curtain, and Marxist philosophy, (16) 21

Isaiah, Book of, image of Yahweh's servant in the, (11) 48-49; sacrifice of atonement in the, (11) 63; temple vision in the, (11) 129

Iserloh, Erwin, (14) 177

Islam, and religious freedom, (18) 64-72

Israel, experience of faith of, (20) 31-33

Israelite "credo", development of the, (20) 29-40

Italian literature, on the homily, (20) 143-150

Italy, communism in, (16) 175-176; modernist movement in, (17) 102-106

Jacob, E., on divine intervention, (11) 71

Jamaa movement, (19) 6

James, St., martyrdom of, (17) 22-23; on pagan practices, (13) 53

Jansenism, Italian, and the Synod of Pistoia, (17) 34-49

Janssens, L., on conscience, (18) 127-128; on faith, (18) 129; on religious freedom, (18) 131-132

Japan, Christianity in present-day, (12) 133-135; (19) 159-165

Jaspers, K., on the bible, (19) 57

Jedin, H., on Vatican Council II, (17) 114, 117

Jerusalem, community of, (12) 6; (17) 21f.; ecumenical institute at, (17) 146-154

Jesus Christ, baptism of, (11) 48; as the center of history, (11) 6, 131; descent into hell of, (11) 125-126, 147-159; divine existence of, (11) 19ff., 50ff., 58-59, 63, 94ff.; in dogmatic tracts, (11) 5-25; in ecumenical dialogue, (14) 47-49, 69; the ensoi of, (11) 9ff.; eschatological significance of, (11) 119-127; freedom of, (11) 92ff.; as an historical figure, (11) 27-46; human beatific vision of, (11) 54, 92ff., 98ff.; human choice of, (11) 50, 55-58; human consciousness of, (11) 91-96; human existence of, (11) 52; integritas of, (11) 59-60; and the Jewish tradition, (20) 16-18; kenosis of, (11) 47-66; as kerygma, (11) 27-46; in the liturgical assembly, (12) 15-17, 19-31, 34f.; in Luther's theology, (14) 14-15, 18-22; New Testament titles applied to, (20) 93-96; obedience of, (11) 56, 64; ontological presence of, (14) 164; and the Pauline tradition, (20) 102-104; pre-existence of, (11) 13, 30; as priest and victim, (11) 68-86; priesthood of, (12) 21ff.; problem of the knowledge of, (11) 91-105; problem of the suffering of, (11) 54f.; resurrection of, (11) 67-87; (13) 6-7; as the sacrificial Lamb, (11) 81-82; as the servant of Yahweh, (11) 48ff.; sinlessness of, (11) 59-60; as the source of a new tradition, (20) 18-19; temptations of, (11) 56; tradition of the sayings of, (20) 62-74; the two natures of, (11) 10, 47ff., 92ff.; universal character of, (19) 81f.; universal kingship of, (11) 107-127, 129-143; (14) 173; as viator and comprehensor, (11) 54-66

Jewish ritual, idea of expiation in, (11) 68-73

Jewish tradition, on Church-State relations, (18) 25ff.; and religious freedom, (18) 21-36

Jews, Nazi execution of the, (17) 14-16; in the Middle Ages, (18) 9f.

Jiménez-Duque, Baldomero, (19) 183

Jiménez-Urresti, Teodoro, (18) 182; on religious freedom, (18) 114, 137-138

Job, (19) 19

John XXIII, Pope, on aid to underdeveloped countries, (15) 46; and

American interest in Vatican Council II, **(17)** 137; on the Church in China, **(13)** 67; on the Church and society, **(15)** 13; on the dignity of man, **(15)** 20-21; on dogmatic formulas, **(14)** 102, 160; and ecumenical relations, **(13)** 87; missionary theology of, **(13)** 16-17, 29, 86, 88, 118, 130; on the pastoral nature of Vatican Council II, **(17)** 112-114, 117; personality of, **(17)** 118; on religious freedom, **(13)** 102; **(18)** 105ff., 124; on the unity of mankind, **(15)** 116

John, St., gospel of, Christ's kenosis in, **(11)** 53; purpose of, **(11)** 79; resurrection of Christ in, **(11)** 74ff.; theology of the Logos in, **(11)** 10f., 19, 48

John Chrysostom, St., on eucharistic cults, **(14)** 174

John Damascene, St., on the Trinity, **(14)** 75

Jolif, J., on non-violence, **(15)** 125-126

Jones, Ernest, psychoanalytic studies of, **(16)** 78

Jordan, W., on religious freedom, **(18)** 112

Jourda, P., on Calvin, **(14)** 39-40

Journet, Charles, missionary theology of, **(13)** 115

Joy, in the liturgical assembly, **(12)** 13-15

Judaism, in the biblical and rabbinic periods, **(18)** 28ff.; the Davidic Messiah in, **(20)** 81-83; idea of death in, **(11)** 81; and religious freedom, **(18)** 21-36

Judaizers, introverted morality of the, **(11)** 85; Paul's dispute with the, **(17)** 21

Julien, David, Church music of, **(12)** 97, 99

Jung, C., criticism of Freud by, **(16)** 86; evolutionary science of, **(16)** 52; on 20th-century myths, **(11)** 150

Jungmann, J., on the liturgical assembly, **(12)** 12

Jurisdictionalism, in Italian Jansenism, **(17)** 35-36

Just war, theory of the, **(15)** 107ff.

Justification, and cosmic christology, **(11)** 126n.; doctrine of, **(14)** 28; in Luther's theology, **(14)** 7, 10, 12, 19

Justin, St., on the eucharist, **(17)** 30; on the generation of the Word, **(11)**

18; on the liturgical assembly, **(12)** 12, 35

Justinian, and monophysitism, **(17)** 156

Kahlefeld, H., Church music of, **(12)** 105

Kamlah, W., on scripture, **(14)** 51

Karmiris, M., on the *Constitution on the Church,* **(14)** 134-137; on the *Decree on Ecumenism,* **(14)** 150

Käsemann, E., on cosmic christology, **(11)** 113; on the historical Jesus, **(11)** 42-43; **(20)** 169

Kaufman, L., S.J., on the African Church, **(13)** 50

Kazem-Bek, A., on the *Constitution on the Church,* **(14)** 144

Kelly, G., on the transplantation of human organs, **(15)** 99

Kenosis, exegetical analysis of, **(11)** 47-53; theological discussion on, **(11)** 53-66

Kenrick, Francis, on episcopal collegiality, **(17)** 139-140

Kerygma, essence of, **(13)** 49; historical roots of, **(11)** 42-44; meaning of, **(11)** 16; and mission **(13)** 113; and the New Testament, **(11)** 28f., 31; **(20)** 98-100; and the Old Testament, **(20)** 96-98; structure of the, **(20)** 90-92

Khomiakov, A., Sobornost doctrine of, **(14)** 143

Khrushchev, Nikita, on the dictatorship of the proletariat, **(16)** 21

Kierkegaard, Soren, on atheism, **(16)** 93; on the demise of Christianity, **(16)** 102-103; on existential conversion, **(15)** 57

Kingdom of God, and liturgical celebration, **(12)** 26

Kingship of Christ, idea of, **(11)** 129-143

Klohr, Olaf, on science and religion, **(16)** 151

Knowledge, absolute, in Hegelian philosophy, **(16)** 133, 135, 151; *a priori,* concept of, **(16)** 115f.; empirical, process of, **(16)** 114ff.; and faith, distinction between, **(15)** 22; in Marxist ideology, **(16)** 174-175; the problem of Christ's, **(11)** 91-105

Knox, R., the sermons of, **(19)** 147f.

Kobayashi, Y., on human knowledge,

Meiji Constitution, and religious liberty, (19) 165

Mejía, Jorge, (14) 179

Menoud, P. H., on the Old Testament, (20) 7

Meouchi, Paul, on religious freedom, (18) 141

Mercier, G., on poverty, (13) 107

Merkle, Sebastian, on Luther, (14) 8-9

Merleau-Ponty, Maurice, atheism of, (16) 41-47; on the Church and revolution, (15) 36

Mersch, E., on Christ's cosmic kingship, (11) 24, 119

Merton, Thomas, spirituality of, (19) 152

Messiah, Jesus as the, (11) 49ff.

Metanoia, in Luther's theology, (14) 26

Metaphysics, and Christ's kingship, (11) 115f.; and the proclamation of God, (16) 95ff.; and revelation, (11) 13-14

Metz, Johannes, (16) 179; on Christian-Marxist dialogue, (16) 165-166; on the future of Christianity, (16) 170-171

Meyendorff, John, on collegiality, (14) 147-150; on communicatio in sacris, (14) 152-154; on eucharistic ecclesiology, (14) 145

Meyer, Albert Cardinal, on episcopal collegiality, (17) 140; on liturgical renewal, (12) 164

Michel, Virgil, O.S.B., and liturgical renewal, (12) 157

Michonneau, G., on parish and mission, (13) 111

Middle Ages, religious freedom in the, (18) 9-12

Miguez, J., on the Decree on Ecumenism, (14) 124

Milton, John, on truth, (15) 23

Ministry, in Calvin's theology, (14) 37, 41

Minocchi, Salvatore, and the Italian modernist movement, (17) 102-103

Miracles, and the French modernist movement, (17) 97

Missiology, theological development of, (13) 81-130

Missionaries, in Africa, (12) 145-146; conflicts among, (13) 18f.; and liturgical renewals, (12) 117; non-Catholic, (14) 104-110; self-re-

nouncement of, (13) 15; spirituality of, (13) 30

Missionary activity, and cultural change, (13) 17-18, 126; in Latin America, (14) 107; and local traditions, (14) 109; models of, (13) 122-123; Moslem attitude toward, (18) 71; nature of, (13) 5f., 32-33; and political intrigue, (13) 13f.; and religious freedom, (18) 75ff.; renewal in, (13) 4f., 11ff., 23-33; task of, (13) 7-8

Missionary government, principles of, (13) 11-33

Missionary institutions, development of, (13) 101-109; foundation of, (13) 98-101

Missions, centralized government for the, (13) 11-33; and Ecclesiology, (13) 81-130; hierarchical power of the, (12) 21-22; and the liturgical assembly, (12) 43; native clergy in the, (13) 20-23; and proselytism, (14) 105-106; religious freedom in the, (18) 56-58; tasks of the, (13) 3-15

Modern society, atheistic mentality of, (16) 100; and Catholic Action, (13) 95-98; Christian position in, (13) 121-122; and Church structure, (13) 151

Modern warfare, in Protestant theology, (15) 122-124; theological discussion on, (15) 105-141

Modernist movement, in England, (17) 101-102; in Italy, (17) 102-106; literature on the, (17) 91-108; reactions against the, (17) 106-108

Mohammed, on religious freedom, (18) 65ff.

Möhler, J., on Luther, (14) 8; on the nature of the Church, (13) 94

Moltmann, Jürgen, (16) 179

Monarchy, in Hegelian philosophy, (16) 133

Monastic life, renewal of, (19) 175-182

Monchanin, J., on mission in India, (13) 123

Monophysitism, and Christ's kenosis, (11) 57-58; in the early Church, (17) 156

Monotheism, in African culture, (13) 51

Monothelitism, and functional revelation, (11) 20

International Publishers of CONCILIUM

ENGLISH EDITION
Paulist Press
Glen Rock, N. J., U.S.A.

Burns & Oates Ltd.
25 Ashley Place
London, S.W.1

DUTCH EDITION
Uitgeverij Paul Brand, N. V.
Hilversum, Netherlands

FRENCH EDITION
Maison Mame
Tours/Paris, France

GERMAN EDITION
Verlagsanstalt Benziger & Co., A.G.
Einsiedeln, Switzerland

Matthias Grunewald-Verlag
Mainz, W. Germany

SPANISH EDITION
Ediciones Guadarrama
Madrid, Spain

PORTUGUESE EDITION
Livraria Morais Editora, Ltda.
Lisbon, Portugal

ITALIAN EDITION
Editrice Queriniana
Brescia, Italy